1

Silkies or Silkie Chickens as pets.

Silkie Bantams facts, raising, breeding, care, food and where to buy all covered.

Including black, white, Chinese and bearded silkie chickens.

by

Elliott Lang

Published by IMB Publishing 2013

Table of Contents

Table of Contents

Table of Contents

Table of Contents

Foreword

There are many conventional reasons to keep chickens, the most practical being a desire to gather eggs or to help you control pests in your garden. Being practical will not be a consideration, however, once you realize how adorable these birds are.

Once you spend even a brief amount of time watching the hatchlings prance around soon after birth and chirping as if to call out your name, your heart will melt.

These small, fluffy birds are so unique that at one time it was a common misconception that they are a chicken / rabbit hybrid. That is, of course, a biological impossibility, but when you pet a Silkie for the first time, the sensation will remind you of running your hand across the finest down.

Don't be surprised to see a different spelling when referring to these lovely creatures. The name "Silkie chicken" is sometimes spelled "Silky chicken" and you may see both referenced in this text.

The feathers of a Silkie lack the little hooks that would hold the individual strands together to create a more rigid structure. Silkies are not only "pet-able," they love to be petted. Many owners say they value their little friends for just how unlike chickens they really are!

Naysayers may protest that owning a pet chicken is just too much trouble, but that's really not the case. They don't have to be walked. They eat all the time, so there's no scheduled feedings, you just have to make clean food and water consistently available.

They don't have to be bathed — although Silkies love a day at the spa — and if you keep your chicken in the house, it can be diapered.

Yes, you can diaper your Silkie and it will let you do it. You can even train your Silkie to wear a harness and use a leash. It's a complete misconception that chickens are unintelligent. They are not capable of understanding complex language, but they do catch on quickly, especially if you reinforce their training with a tasty treat — a grape or maybe a nice piece of banana.

But wait. Don't chickens eat corn and grain and stuff? Yes. But they will also eat table scraps and insects — really about anything, and you can buy as much as 50 lbs. (22.6 kg) of commercial chicken feed for $20 - $25 (£13.18 -£16.48.) That's enough to last a couple of chickens 3 to 4 months!

If your goal in investigating Silkie chickens is to expose your children to the whole life cycle from fertilized egg to grown bird, you're looking at a two-month period of incubation and brooding — again at minimal expense — followed by a typical lifespan of 9 years.

In that period, your children will not only enjoy the loving affection of a sweet-tempered pet, but they will also learn a great deal about animal husbandry.

This book provides a comprehensive overview of Silkie chickens, including a discussion of their housing needs outside and inside.

Common illnesses are described, along with daily care routines, feeding and grooming requirements. The text also touches on the intricacies of entering your chickens for judging in poultry shows. There are links to relevant websites throughout, and a compilation of such reference sources at the end of the book.

Never bring a pet of any kind home without first making all the necessary preparations for their proper care and feeding. In these pages, you'll find out everything you need to know about locating, adopting, and making a Silkie chicken part of your family.

But be warned, it's extremely difficult to stop at just one Silkie! You're about to meet the most charming and social of all chicken breeds — and, like most of us who have had Silkies in our lives, you'll fall in love with their whimsical personalities and loving ways. There's simply no other chicken out there like a Silkie. Read on to find out why.

Chapter 1 - An Introduction to Silkie Chickens

It's almost impossible to see a Silkie chicken and not be intrigued. The downy quality of their unusual feathers and their showy crests lead many people to say these birds wear "wigs." Add in the plumy leg feathers reminiscent of old-fashioned ladies' pantalettes, and a Silkie is an irresistibly cute bird.

You may also see the breed referred to as the Japanese Silkie chicken or the Chinese Silkie chicken.

The real plus is that the Silkie chicken breed has the personality to go with their good looks. Silkies like people, and they like to interact with us in their often quizzical and endearing way.

1. History of Silkie Chickens

These unique chickens are aptly named. Touch one for the first time, and you'll feel like you're running your hand over the softest silk. Docile by nature, and so small in size they're sometimes mistakenly referred to as bantams, Silkies are charming companions, and superb show fowl. (Silkies are called Silkie bantams in the U.S., but not in the UK)

It's likely the breed originated somewhere in Southeast Asia. In the 13th century, the Italian traveler Marco Polo wrote about unusual chickens he encountered that were, to his eye, "furry." His comments are believed to be the first written reference to the Silkie breed.

A more comprehensive description was penned in 1599 by another Italian, the naturalist Ulisse Aldrovandi from the University of Bologna. He described the birds as "wool-bearing chickens," and likened their "hair" to that of a black cat.

The most probable explanation for the appearance of Silkie chickens in Europe is that they, like so many foreign luxuries of the 16th century, made their way west along the Silk Route from Asia. In the United States, the breed was admitted to the American Poultry Association's *Standard of Perfection* during its first year of publication in 1874.

The Silkie's appearance has spawned a lot of tall tales, like the absurd notion put forth by breeders in Holland that the birds are the offspring of rabbits and chickens. Without question, however, there is something whimsical about a Silkie with its slightly determined expression and strutting walk.

These beautiful and personable birds are one of the most popular of all ornamental poultry breeds. They make excellent pets — in the backyard, and sometimes even in the house — and are highly valued as show birds.

2. General Characteristics of Silkie Chickens

Silkie chickens are strikingly handsome fowl. In addition to their soft plumage, Silkies have blue meat, blue bones, and blue earlobes. Unlike most chickens, they have five toes on each foot and their legs and feet are feathered. They cannot fly, a fact that, along with their placid nature, makes them very easy to control and contain.

One of the most beguiling aspects of their appearance is their "crests," which are tufts of feathers that sit jauntily atop their heads. As the crests grow, they have a tendency to curl down toward the bird's face. The crest disguises the fact that a Silkie's skull is vaulted.

In a show chicken, this vaulting will actually be a visible arch on top of the head, which creates vulnerability. Silkies are prone to developing a condition called "water on the brain" (discussed later in this book) and they can be killed or severely impaired neurologically by a solid peck on the head by another bird.

The crest can also interfere with a Silkie's vision, a problem handled in show chickens in a variety of unique ways from simple hairpins to stylist tape and even decorative elastic hair ties. (See Showing Silkies for more information.) For Silkies kept as pets, it may be necessary to carefully clip the crest so the birds can see where they're going!

Averaging 1.5 – 4 pounds (3.3 – 8.8 kg) in weight, a Silkie chicken's lifespan is typically 9 years. They are not high maintenance pets, requiring little grooming, although show chickens get a lot more "fluffing" up before they enter the ring.

Silkies are friendly birds that enjoy being handled to the point of actually craving attention. They can be very affectionate and loyal. If handled gently from an early age, a Silkie will be a devoted pet and companion, and will even be agreeable to learning tricks as long as there's something in it for him — like a favorite treat.

A hardy breed with a resilient constitution, Silkies are fairly active birds and like to run around and scratch for their meals, but they are not noisy and can be successfully kept in urban settings if zoning ordinances allow for a backyard coop. (For more information on the legal considerations of keeping backyard chickens, see Chapter 2.)

To be healthy and happy, Silkies will need a place to roam around without fear of predators. Conventional wisdom recommends a space 3 feet wide and 8 feet long (approximately 1 meter by 2.4 meters) for a maximum of four chickens. (To learn more about building chicken enclosures, see Chapter 2.)

3. Breed Improvements and Show Popularity

There have been significant improvements in the breed over the past three decades, which has led to a proliferation of new colorations, and a gradual increase in the amount of feathering on the legs. Much of this activity has been in response to the growing popularity of Silkie chickens as show animals.

Silkie chickens are a favorite choice for young people participating in showing animals through 4H, a global youth development program now found in more than 70 countries.

The extreme docility of the Silkie, and the ease with which it can be kept, even in an urban setting, makes it an excellent choice for kids who are not in a position to keep larger show livestock like cattle, sheep, goats, or pigs.

4. Egg Production and Use as Meat

Silkie hens are incredibly "broody" and will mother any baby animal of any species that follows them around. This motherly instinct does not extend to high egg production, however. At most, expect to get 3 eggs a week out of a Silkie hen (approximately 90-120 eggs per year).

To encourage greater egg production, gather the eggs as soon as possible after laying. If you do allow a Silkie to hatch a clutch of eggs, expect about 6-8 chicks. Silky chicken eggs are small and cream colored.

People who raise game birds like quail or partridges will often keep a flock of Silkies to use them as living incubators. These hens love to brood so much, they'll nest even when they don't have any eggs, leading many enthusiasts to laughingly say a Silkie will "hatch rocks!" The phrase "mother hen" could have been coined exclusively for these chickens.

Interestingly, when raising her own chicks, a Silkie hen is not a single mother. Silkie roosters have their own share of the breed's strong maternal instinct. Males are extremely gentle with the chicks, bringing them food, and spending time with them in the chicken yard, clearly babysitting.

It is extremely rare for Silkies to be raised for their meat, which, due to its dark blue color, can be visually off putting. The meat is edible, but people who have tried it report that it has a "gamey" flavor. It is used in Asian cultures where it is believed to have curative powers, but at least in the Western world, these birds are primarily pets and show animals.

Understanding the Silkie's Special Feather Structure

Birds are the only animals on earth that have feathers; the epidermal growths that enable the vast majority of avian species to fly. Chickens, however, are not really flight birds. They are part of a broader family of birds known as "poultry" that also includes turkeys, guineas, and ducks. These birds are well adapted to living on the ground, although hunters will tell you that wild ducks are some of the best flyers around.

However, if you really look at poultry, you'll see that their beaks are designed for pecking at the ground, and their feet are made primarily for walking.

Chickens do roost at night, wrapping their feet around perches, but they spend their days strutting and scratching around the yard looking for insects and enjoying their dirt baths. When startled, chickens can fly short distances, but they're just as likely to take off running.

Birds Have Two Types of Feathers

Silkie chickens can't fly at all, and their feathers are very different. Most birds, including poultry, have two types of feathers.

- **Vaned feathers** covering the exterior of the body. Visually, a vaned feather is what we think of when we hear the word "feather."

- **Down feathers**
are softer, and lie
underneath these
more rigid
structures. Down
is soft and fluffy,
and is the first
bodily covering a
baby chick has
when it hatches.

In popular human
use, vaned
feathers are
largely
ornamental.

Just imagine a
feather tucked at a cocky angle in the band of a hat and you'll get

the idea. Traditionally, down feathers have been used as padding and insulation, for instance in pillows and mattresses, or in jackets.
(The down used for such purposes comes from water fowl, and the practice has been increasingly discontinued in modern times due to its association with animal cruelty.)

Typical Feather Structure vs. Silkie Feathers

A typical vaned feather has a central "shaft." This is the hard "line" that divides the feather into two parts. The vanes extend from either side of the shaft. Each vane is made up of a series of parallel branches called barbs.

Each barb, in turn, has shorter branches or extensions called barbules. These minute structures are hooked, and hold the feather together, making it rigid, but exceptionally light and thus well adapted for flight.

A Silkie chicken's feathers have no functioning barbicels, so the individual strands of the feather are not held together. Each of these strands is 1-2 inches (50-75mm) in length and very soft. This structural difference is what makes a Silkie look "furry" or "hairy."

Molting and Dust

All chickens produce "dust" as a natural part of their feathering cycle. This is an on-going, year-round process that escalates in the spring and fall. The bulk of the dust comes from the growth of new feathers. As the feather shafts grow, they also flake off. Any time a chicken loses a feather, the structure is replaced, and therefore some dust is always present.

In the fall, however, chickens molt, meaning they lose the bulk of their feathers and replace them. This can be a startling process for new chicken owners who aren't prepared for just how "plucked" and "naked" their birds will look. Obviously then, molting is a period of high dust production.

Young birds, including Silkies, also molt as they lose their juvenile feathers. This is simply a part of the maturation process, and not a sign of disease. There is no molting of adults in the spring, but there can be accelerated feather growth, which also leads to more dust being shed.

5. Types of Silkie Chickens

Silkie chickens come in bearded and non-bearded varieties. The "beard" is a small ruffle or mass of feathers just under the beak and around the face. The wattle, the fleshy lob hanging from the chicken's neck, is different in each variety:

- A non-bearded Silkie has large wattles, hanging 25mm-40mm (1" – 1.5") below the beak, with smaller wattles on a hen.

- A bearded Silkie has small wattles, hanging 5mm (less than .25") below the beak, surrounded by the fluffy beard.

Both bearded and non-bearded varieties have the trademark feathery crest, and both have a comb atop the head. Silkies have only a rose or cushion comb, however, which resembles a wart on the bird's forehead.

Accepted Silkie chicken colors include: black, blue, bluff, white, partridge, splash, gray, lavender, red, porcelain, and cuckoo. (The last four colors are not accepted for show.)

Chapter 2 - Keeping Backyard Silkie Chickens

Silkie chickens are not a breed kept for their ability to produce a lot of eggs, nor are they kept as "fryers." In theory, chickens can help keep insects out of your garden, although they very well may peck up the tender shoots of young plants along with the grubs.

Chicken manure and cast off straw are a superb addition to a compost heap, so in that sense, keeping backyard chickens is environmentally sound.

Primarily, however, Silkie chickens serve as pets and show animals, providing companionship and entertainment for their humans. Additionally, owning and caring for pet chickens is an educational experience for children, especially those living in urban areas, who would otherwise have no chance to explore animal husbandry.

If you are allowed to keep Silkie chickens as pets in your area, you have many decisions to make regarding how your chickens will be housed — decisions that must be made and implemented BEFORE you bring baby chicks home.

1. Legal Considerations

There is no single answer regarding laws regulating the keeping of poultry. The provisions are usually contained under city zoning ordinances, and range from an outright prohibition, to a limit on the number of chickens allowed, to a ban on roosters only. If you plan to keep a house chicken, the "governing" authority may be your own homeowners association.

For chicken laws and ordinances in the United States, the best online source is BackYardChickens.com/atype/3/Laws

This well-maintained website is consistently updated, and contains a section on "new laws and ordinances." If you cannot find an answer there, your best option is to call the city office in your town or municipality. They will direct you to the correct office, which will likely be the animal control department.

In Great Britain, poultry owners with 50 or more birds must enroll in the Great Britain Poultry Register, which became active in December 2005. Its purpose is primarily to aid in disease tracking and control.

Local ordinances and codes affect pet chicken ownership more directly than any national statute. A housing development, for instance, might have covenants or codes that exclude poultry and livestock. The best option is to consult local authorities before acquiring a pet chicken.

2. Building Chicken Enclosures

Unless you decided to keep your Silkie chicken in the house (which is a viable option discussed fully in Chapter 3), you have a lot to do before you bring your new bird home. It's a mistake to think that you can just buy a cage, stick it in the backyard, and put the Silkie inside.

Chickens have very specific needs when it comes to their enclosures.

Location, Location, Location

Your first decision in housing chickens is to choose where your enclosure will be located. You want a spot with plenty of sunshine, but also lots of available shade. Don't select a low-lying area. It's not healthy for chickens to be forced to wade in standing water.

Once you have decided where the enclosure will be placed, then you can determine which living arrangement is best suited to your property and to your goals for having the chickens in the first place. There are four basic ways to keep chickens:

- Confined to a coop with a small, attached yard or run.
- Free ranging over a yard with a coop for nighttime roosting.
- Limited ranging, which is a combination of both approaches.*
- Chicken tractors or moveable coops.

(* In limited ranging, a coop or hen house is surrounded by a much larger yard or run so that the chickens have a degree of movement similar to that available in free ranging, but still within the confines of a protective structure.)

Space is an Important Consideration

Providing adequate space is essential for the health of your birds, regardless of the type of enclosure you choose to use.

A single chicken needs about 4 sq. ft. (0.37m^2) of room per section of any part of its enclosure. For instance:

- If you want to raise three chickens, you will need 12 sq. feet (1.11 m^2) of space in a coop.

- If you add a "run" or "yard" to that coop, that area should also be 12 sq. feet (1.11 m^2).

Remember, overcrowding not only stresses chickens and leads to squabbling in the flock, but it also increases the chances of disease or illness spreading. Don't forget that chickens are very messy birds. The more of them you try to cram in a small space, the more difficult you will make it for yourself to adequately clean and maintain the coop.

Other Important Decisions About Your Coop

You will also need to make decisions about:

- ***Height of the coop***. Although chickens lay their eggs in nests, they roost at night on perches and will need adequate headroom as well as a good distance off the floor for ease of cleaning. Remember, you have to be able to get into the coop to maintain the area. NEVER put feeders or waterers under the roosts.

- ***Roosting*** - It's especially important for Silkie chickens to be able to roost since they have feathered feet. Show birds' feet must be kept clean at all times, but no Silkie should be allowed to wander about on a dirty floor, in standing water, or in mud. Dirty feet invite parasites and infections.

- ***Ventilation***. You don't want a coop to be drafty, but neither do you want heat and moisture to build up. That's an open invitation to disease and to a wide variety of parasites. If possible, create cross ventilation, which enhances cooling, decreases odor, and provides maximum drying. (See the next section on Climate Control.)

- ***Flooring***. It's important not to make the floor of a coop slippery, but neither do you want to use materials that will rot or harbor odors. Most people opt for either dirt or wood floors because the wood dries easily if the ventilation in the coop is good. The floor will be covered with bedding, which absorbs urine, feces, and spilled water.

- **Lighting**. Managing stress with chickens is always a major consideration, and hens do not like to feel completely closed in and trapped. Natural light also allows the chickens to keep a regular schedule of waking and sleeping. Your coop needs windows.

- **Nest boxes**. Even though Silkies are not good layers, they are incredibly broody and love to nest. They will sleep on their perches at night, but clean, dry nest boxes filled with straw or wood shavings will make your hens very happy, and even with Silkies, you should get about 3 eggs a week.

You will want a completely constructed coop and all the necessary supplies in place, so your Silkies can come home to an environment tailor-made for their needs. Then they can become acclimated with a minimum amount of stress.

Climate Control

Silkie chickens like to have access to sunlight, but they are sensitive to high temperatures. It is essential that they have cool water and a shady place to get in out of the heat.

If the temperatures in your area routinely reach 100 degrees F (37.8 C) or more in the summer, your Silkies will need more cooling. Most growers use misting units and a fan, but it is not unheard of for a chicken house to be air-conditioned in very hot climates.

Chickens do not sweat, they pant to cool off. When the ambient temperature rises too high, they simply cannot stay ahead of the rising mercury. Water misting systems are not expensive, and can be obtained online or in big box gardening stores for $25 to $50 (£16.48 to £32.96).

Some have fans included, or you can use a simple box fan to move the lightly misted air. This is not a luxury for your Silkies, but can be a real lifesaver during brutal summer months.

Finding Plans to Build a Chicken Coop and Associated Costs

The Internet is full of plans for chicken coop designs. An excellent source for "do it yourself" builders is BackyardChickens.com, and don't forget YouTube. For many people, it's much easier to visualize the finished product when they're watching the process as it unfolds.

Sites like CleanCoops.com sell coop plans for download for about $35 (£23.07), while offering building and cleaning tips to their customers. Construction costs vary by material cost and complexity, but on chicken discussion forums most owners ballpark a coop with attached yard in the $200 to $400 (£131.83 to £263.66) range. These custom designed structures tend to be larger than commercial coops that can be purchased and assembled.

If, however, you are not the "handy" sort and want to buy a ready-made coop, there are options like ChickenCoopSource.com and other retail venues online and off. Coops can be purchased as "kits," which range from small "starter" units for approximately $230 to $250 (£151.60 to £164.79) all the way up to decorator "cottage" coops costing as much as $2000 (£1318.30).

In the "real" world of purchases, there are many options for the prospective chicken owner. Coops are not complex structures, and any good carpenter can easily construct one, although labor costs will be added to materials.

Readymade coops can be found at many feed and hardware stores, especially in rural areas, and in some areas even big box retail giants like Walmart have chicken enclosures for sale.

A coop is necessary in each of the enclosure arrangements, and is the primary cost consideration. If you free-range your chickens, the coop is all you'll need. If, however, you construct a limited ranging environment, you will need to factor in the costs of the larger surrounding "yard" or "run" as well. These costs can vary widely, especially if you build the run yourself or hire a carpenter to do it.

Commercially produced chicken runs, which are essentially rectangular wood frames of varying sizes with chicken wire walls start at $300 to $500 (£197.75 to £329.58) for an enclosure that is approximately 4' x 3' (1.22m x 0.91m).

At just 12 sq. ft. (1.11 m^2), however, this would only accommodate about 3 chickens. For a limiting ranging set up, you would require a fenced area 2 to 3 times that size.

3. Keeping Your Chickens Confined to a Coop

Confining your birds to a structure that keeps them safe from predators and limits their movements to a given area has many advantages. Since chickens like to scratch and hunt for their food, confined birds rely exclusively on their keepers to meet all their nutritional needs.

Also note that within a week, any amount of yard included in a confined chicken coop will be reduced to bare ground. Not only will the chickens have eaten every blade of grass, but they will also take regular dirt baths, which discourages any re-growth.

(Dirt baths are the birds' natural way of controlling parasites and should be encouraged.)

Special care must be taken when confining chickens not to create overcrowding, which is a major stressing agent for poultry. This may cause the birds to become combative with one another, while others will die prematurely.

The recommended space for a confined chicken coop with a yard is an area 8 feet long by 3 feet wide (2.44m by 0.9m) for no more than 3 chickens.

4. Free Ranging with Nighttime Roosting

Chickens that are allowed to "free range" can roam around a designated (and usually un-caged) area all day looking for the things they like to eat including grass and insects. This certainly allows the birds to manage their own diet in a more natural and spontaneous way in addition to the feed given to them by their keepers.

At night, the birds retire to a coop for roosting, and often they are locked in or otherwise secured against predators at that time. Typically, the chickens are released early in the morning when they are given their first feeding of the day.

The biggest disadvantage to free ranging your chickens is that the birds are left vulnerable to a wide range of predators including wild animals and domestic dogs and cats.

5. The Compromise Solution of Limited Ranging

As is the case with confining chickens to a coop, a limited ranging solution creates an enclosure within an enclosure. A small coop with a limited yard is set inside a bigger enclosed area with or without a roof. (Hawks and other birds of prey will snatch chickens, so it's usually a good idea to have a mesh top on your chicken yard if possible.)

If you have the room to create a limited ranging environment, your chickens will be able to spend their days scratching, pecking, and bathing in the dirt, which they will enjoy, but you will have the option of confining them to a smaller area as the need arises, and locking them in the coop at night for their safety.

Also, given the available space, you can raise more chickens with greater safety.

6. Chickens Drive "Tractors?"

Not exactly. A chicken "tractor" is a movable chicken coop. This arrangement lets you relocate the coop, which gives the chickens greater access to fresh grass and insect populations. When one area of yard starts to wear down, the coop is moved to a new spot.

Obviously, this method requires a large piece of property, but it does carry the advantage of confinement and protection. Again, however, overcrowding will be a major cautionary consideration.

In shopping for or building a chicken tractor, remember that this is essentially an "all in one" efficiency apartment for chickens. The unit will include a coop with nesting boxes and roosts, and an attached, covered, yard or run.

While some tractors are constructed on axles with wheels, a "sled" approach may be more practical to meet the goal of actually getting the chickens on the ground.

(Note that units with wheels may be easier to physically move, whereas movable coops built as sleds have to be dragged with a garden tractor or farm "mule.")

Many ready-made chicken tractors place the coop itself on the ground. This is a waste of space and counter to the chickens' natural preferences. If you want to use a chicken tractor, find one where the coop is raised at least 20 inches. This is an added protection against predators, and it increases the amount of ground space where the birds can roam and scratch.

A good size tractor would be 5' wide (1.52 m) and 6-7' (1.82 – 2.13 m) long. This would provide 30 to 35 sq. ft. (2.79 to 3.25 m^2), enough for 7 to 8 Silkies since they are small-bodied birds.

In addition to a raised coop with nesting boxes, the tractor should have some type of sunshade over the main yard, and secure doors or panels that allow the coop and boxes to be cleaned, and the food and water to be changed.

The frequency with which the tractor is moved is entirely dependent on how quickly the birds strip the ground at any given location.

Chicken tractors have become especially popular in urban and suburban settings, and they are often rotated over home gardens where the chickens naturally till the soil and help keep the insect population down.

Chicken tractors can also be purchased commercially or built from plans readily available online. (See "How to Build a Movable Chicken Coop or Chicken Tractor" at http://smallfarm.about.com/od/farminfrastructure/ss/sbscoopbuild .htm or use your favorite search engine to search for "plans to build a chicken tractor.")

Retail chicken tractors cost anywhere from $500 to $1000 (£329.58 to £659.15). To build a 35 sq. ft. (3.25 m^2) chicken tractor, you would need approximately $300 (£197.75) worth of parts and materials.

7. Keeping Chickens in the House

Yes, some people do keep their chickens in the house, a topic discussed more fully in Chapter 3. Under those circumstances, and outfitted with poultry "diapers," the birds can "free range" indoors.

This is, however, a completely different environment than that to which a chicken is accustomed, and care will have to be taken to accommodate the bird's natural desires to scratch, peck, and bathe in the dirt. Silkies are so docile, they will submit to being "walked" on a leash, which is a safe way, with observation, to give them access to the outdoors.

Indoor chickens will still want to roost at night, so an appropriate cage with perches will be necessary, and Silkies love to nest. Of course, if they have the option of nesting on a nice, soft sofa cushion over a straw lined box, don't be surprised. Chickens — especially personable and affectionate birds like Silkies — get used to living in the "big house" very quickly!

8. Taking Precautions Against Predators

Regardless of the type of enclosure you use to house your Silkie chickens, take all the necessary precautions against predators. In an outdoor setting, this means using chicken wire or hardware cloth extending at least 6 inches (15.24 cm) out from the edge of the enclosure to discourage digging. It's also a good idea to have wire on the top of the enclosure to prevent birds of prey, like hawks, from snatching one of your chickens.

The animals you will be guarding against include, but are not limited to: raccoons, coyotes, foxes, weasels, skunks, hawks, owls, opossums, bobcats, snakes, and even squirrels.

Some of these creatures are after eggs only, but many will also kill the chickens themselves. When dealing with raccoons in particular, no latch is strong enough. Lock your coop up at night and make sure all the windows and other points of entry are completely secure.

Don't fall into the trap of trusting domestic dogs and cats around your chickens, even your own pet. In some cases domestic animals just ignore chickens, but even in play, the birds can wind up on the losing end of a confrontation. Chickens are so susceptible to stress that a dog can torment one to death thinking the whole business is a game.

Chickens are not without their own responsibility in these matters. Terms like "pecking order" and "pecked to death" developed for a reason. Hens can be highly territorial and have been known to harass barn cats — until the cat puts an end to the matter.

The best rule of thumb is to assume that anything that can kill or eat your chicken will.

Chapter 3 - Your Silkie Chicken as Part of the Family

People who say that they cannot imagine having a real attachment to a chicken haven't met a Silkie. These soft, beautiful little birds have a unique charm that sets them apart in the world of poultry. It's for this reason that they make excellent pets.

Silkies are also perfect show animals, and work well with young children participating in judged events for the first time. It's simply impossible not to fall in love with a Silkie, so it's important to understand what the new member of your family needs in the way of your care, help, protection, attention, and affection.

1. Silkie Chickens and Other Chickens in Outside Enclosures

If you are introducing Silkie chickens to an existing flock of larger chickens, it's best to first let the birds get to know each other through some kind of open barrier, for instance a common fence. That allows both sides to check each other out and acclimate, while making overt aggression impossible. After approximately a week, the Silkies can be turned loose within the larger poultry community with supervision, just to make certain there are no altercations.

It may be a good idea to give the Silkie a smaller, individual coop of their own just to ensure peaceful relations, especially if the Silkies are young birds. This does not have to be a long-term arrangement, however, and may not be necessary at all. Silkies do very well with larger chicken breeds, and there are rarely any major problems with integrating them.

2. Silkie Chickens and Other Pets

Having chickens around other domestic animals, especially cats, can be an "iffy" situation. Some cats completely ignore chickens, while others will harass and attack them. (Never trust a cat around a baby chick. The feline instinct is just too strong to resist the temptation.) The caution extends to dogs as well. Often domestic animals think they're just playing with chickens, but in the process the birds can succumb to stress, or can be wounded enough to bleed.

If a chicken is injured by another pet, the real threat to the bird's life may come from its own kind. If other hens see blood on a bird that has been hurt, they may well peck the animal to death. If one of your chickens is wounded in any way, segregate that bird from the flock for its own safety.

31

The general consensus of opinion is that chickens should be kept away from other pets. If you intend to keep your Silkie inside, especially in an apartment setting where segregation isn't easily managed, owning a chicken might not be a good option until you have more room.

3. Keeping "House" Chickens

Obviously chickens aren't the right pet for everyone. Even docile and charming birds like Silkies can still be loud at times, especially if they're scared. If you live in an apartment, it would be best to get a hen, since roosters will crow eventually — and usually at just the time you don't want them to. Also, all poultry, regardless of how they are housed, are messy.

Your bird's cage will need to be cleaned often, and if you are raising the chicken for show, precautions have to be taken to keep the animal as clean as possible. Once a chicken's feathers are stained, it's very hard to get them clean again, especially if your bird is pure white.

It's important to make sure you are allowed to keep a chicken as a pet in your area. You will need to check your town's zoning ordinances, especially if you intend to have a rooster, and also, if applicable, the by-laws of your homeowners association.

If you have other pets in the home, be realistic about how they will get along with a pet chicken. The leading cause of death among house chickens is injury after being attacked by another domestic animal, usually a dog or cat.

The Chicken's Cage

The smallest cage you can use for a Silkie kept in a home is 2 sq. ft. (.0.19 m^2) The chicken must be allowed out during the day to play. Note that you CAN NOT use cedar shavings bought at pet stores as chicken bedding. They are TOXIC to chickens.

The bird's food and water dish will need to hang on the side of the cage, since chickens like to scratch and easily contaminate their own bowls with feces and other material. Be prepared for the mess when your bird scratches bedding out the catch and into the surrounding area.

Chickens like a nesting box, but they sleep on roosts. Be sure the cage is tall enough to accommodate a bar about mid-way up for this purpose and be careful not to position food and water dishes under the roost.

Silkies are an excellent choice as house chickens because they are much quieter than other breeds and are well known for being calm and friendly. Hens normally squawk when they lay eggs, but Silkies are not good layers, rarely producing more than 3 eggs a week.

How Many Indoor Silkies?

Out of fairness to the chickens, you have to be guided by a realistic assessment of your available space. Overcrowding is one of the leading causes of death for chickens kept in coops.

Silkies living in the lap of luxury inside the house are not going to be any happier if they're left in a small cage all day and not given enough time and space to run around and be chickens.

Given these considerations, and the fact that Silkies love human interaction, it is not cruel to keep a single Silkie as a pet in an indoor setting. For most homes, two indoor chickens is the limit. If you are away from home for long periods of time, try to keep two Silkies since they do need companionship.

Food and Water

Fresh water should be made available at all times. Chickens are omnivores, and will eat almost anything, including table snacks.

When they are allowed to scratch and peck in the yard, no insect is safe. Consider buying bags of small crickets sold in pet stores as lizard food for your chicken. You may want to dispense these one at a time rather than have bugs running around your house.

Once your chicken has learned to recognize the bag of crickets, however, there won't be any problem about one getting away. Many chicken owners say that giving their birds cricket treats is one of their favorite "games" because it's so much fun to watch the speed and accuracy with which the Silkie will go after the tasty, hopping morsel and make short work of it.

For the most part, you will be feeding your chicken nutritional pellets or crumbles augmented with some cracked grains. (For more information on this topic, refer to Chapter 5 - Daily Care of Silkie Chickens.)

Chicken Diapers

Diapers are a must for chickens kept in the house because the birds cannot be reliably housebroken. Some people claim to have taught their Silkies to use newspapers spread on the floor.

Generally, a chicken's tail will twitch before the animal relieves itself, so very vigilant owners could, in theory, direct the chicken to an appropriate place to do its "business." This process would have to start in infancy, and would be highly time consuming, but some Silkie owners online claim they have been successful.

The vast majority, however, prefer to use chicken diapers which are similar to products used by parrot owners. The garments fit neatly over the chicken's vent to catch waste materials and are often colorful and fun.

A Silkie will generally wear a "small" diaper. The pouches of the diaper are lined in vinyl, and are adjustable with velcro snaps. Most cost approximately $25 to $30 (£16.48 to £19.77) for the protective cover.

You will want more than one diaper, since you will basically be emptying and washing a pouch that has captured the bird's waste. This is not typically an arrangement similar to a human baby's diaper where a pad is soiled and then removed and discarded. The majority of chicken diapers on the market do not use a pad, and are well designed, and do not tend to leak. There are, however, some specialty products like those made by WorkingWings.com that allow the pouch to be lined with newspaper, scrap fabric, human diapers, or even sanitary napkins.

Harnesses and Leashes

Chicken harnesses are designed to fit over and around the bird's wings, providing a point of attachment for a leash in the center of the bird's back.

Some diaper holders serve the double function of acting as a harness. This will allow you to take your Silkie outside to enjoy scratching and pecking for insects in green grass, and to "bathe" in the dirt, which not only gives the chicken pleasure, but helps to control parasites like mites.

In the beginning, let your chicken wear the harness for short periods of time without the leash attached. Next, allow the bird to wear the harness and let it drag the leash. This will enable the chicken to get used to the weight of the lead.

Be careful that there is nothing in the area on which the leash will catch or snag, as this experience could well frighten the chicken off the whole process for good.

When the bird is used to both the harness and the leash, hold the leash, step as far away from the chicken as the lead allows, and hold out a treat. Get the chicken used to walking toward you, gently applying pressure if they head off in the wrong direction.

Ultimately they will understand the concept of the leash and will allow you to suggest course corrections, but for the most part, "walking" a chicken is more a matter of you following the bird with the lead held slack while the chicken investigates. The harness and leash keep you in control of the situation, however, preventing the bird from wandering off. Fortunately, Silkies do not fly, so that is not an issue.

The Importance of Dust Baths for House Chickens

Chickens don't take water baths on their own, but they do love to use dust for their grooming. Like many animals that roll in dirt, the chickens are using a natural means of controlling parasites like mites, but the dust also removes excess oil from their feathers.

Depending on the time of year, the dust can either help the bird to stay cool, or to provide warmth. Regardless of the functionality of the dust bath, the chickens are obviously having a good time because a hen can kick up a regular cloud of dirt.

If you don't take your chicken outside at all, get a good-sized pan and fill it with play sand a couple of inches (50.8 cm) deep. Put the chicken in the pan and prepare for the mess! It's best to put a layer or two of newspaper down around the pan to catch cast off sand, but Silkies are so cute when they're stirring up dust, it's almost impossible not to enjoy this important ritual with them.

Toys for Your Chicken

As mentioned above, using live crickets as a nutritional snack and a toy for your pet Silkie is an excellent idea. Chickens are much more intelligent than people realize. They have keen vision, and spend a lot of their time searching for their food.

Some chickens are more receptive to learning tricks than others, and, like most animals, must be induced with treats to complete the desired action. Games of "catch" and "fetch" are the easiest, but with patience, many owners have successfully taught their birds to manipulate objects with their beaks or feet, and to respond to spoken commands.

(In general, however, chickens are not good with complex language, and respond much more readily to visual cues and treats.)

Silkie Chickens Love Attention

One thing Silkie owners love about their birds is just how "un-chicken-like" they really are. Silkies enjoy being handled. They welcome interaction. They are loving and affectionate and will want to be part of the family. Don't get a Silkie with the idea that it's just going to sit in its cage. These beautiful little birds make wonderful family pets, and they thrive on love, attention, and care.

Chapter 4 - Buying Silkie Chicks or Fertilized Eggs

As with any pet, when the time comes to buy your Silkie chicken, the questions are fundamentally the same. "Where do I buy the chickens? How many should I get? Should I buy eggs or live chicks? If I buy chicks, what age should they be?"

You need to have considered these questions before you answer a "Silkie chickens for sale" ad. Let's start with a consideration of quantity.

1. How Many Chickens Can You Keep?

It cannot be stressed strongly enough that overcrowding is the number one cause of stress-related death in chickens. People who are new to poultry keeping always underestimate how much room their birds will need.

If you will be keeping your Silky chickens outside in some type of coop arrangement (see Chapter 2 - Keeping Backyard Silkie Chickens for more information on enclosures) the minimum space required per bird is 4 sq. ft. $(0.37m^2)$

House chickens are, of course, a completely different matter. Most people, no matter how much they love Silkies, don't want a flock of chickens running around the living room.

If you are in an apartment, two birds is likely to be the upper limit. You have to consider not just available space, but the rules of your apartment complex or homeowners association as well as being considerate of your neighbors.

Silkie chickens are much quieter than most poultry, but they can still squawk and fuss if they're startled or frightened. If you live in an apartment, don't even consider getting a rooster.

2. Fertilized Eggs, Chicks, or Grown Birds

To understand more about the process involved in incubating eggs and brooding chicks, see Chapter 7 - Breeding and Raising Silkie Chickens.

The most important thing to realize is that if you start with eggs, you will need an incubator, and it will be 19 to 21 days before your chicks hatch.

Twenty-four hours after they hatch, the chicks will need to be transferred into a brooder, where they will remain for at least a month, or until their adult feathers have come in and they can regulate their own body temperature. Brooding will also be necessary if you buy live chicks locally or online. (Chapter 7 also contains information on what is involved in brooding chicks.)

If you have a source for acquiring a young chicken, you can skip the work involved in the incubation and brooding process. Silkies are such friendly and affectionate birds, it's possible to develop a relationship and rapport with one regardless of its age. Just make sure that you have everything you need in place before you bring your new pet home.

If you live in an area where you have access to farms and breeders, you can pick up a pair of pet-quality adult Silkie bantam chickens for approximately $20 to $120 (£13.18 to £131.83) per pair. (Show quality birds are more expensive and prices vary widely.)

The American Silkie Bantam Club will provide a list of Silkie chicken breeders in your area if you contact the group via their website at americansilkiebantamclub.org. In the UK, contact The Silkie Club of Great Britain.

3. Buying Silkie Chicks Online

When you buy Silkie chickens online, the hatchery will provide a list of the varieties in which they deal, referring to color and, if applicable, the beard. So, you might see a listing for a "Bearded Blue Silkie Bantam Chicken Hen." There should be a photograph of the bird to give you an idea of the quality of chickens offered by the hatchery in question.

Expect to see listings for: black Silkie chickens, white Silkie chickens, bantam Silkies, blue Silkie chickens, Silky fowl, blue Silkie bantams, buff Silkies, baby Silkie chickens, bearded Silkie chickens, buff Silkie bantams, and similar phrases.

Policy statements will be attached to the listing page. For instance, "Five bird minimum for each breed variety and color. We ship straight run chicks at 1 days of age. Package will arrive at your post office in 2 to 3 days."

(Note that many breeders will not ship chicks under 4 months of age and many will not send the birds by mail during the hot summer months.)

A "straight run" is a group of chicks that have not been sorted by gender. Do not believe a hatchery that claims to guarantee the sex of the Silkie chicks they ship. It's impossible to determine gender for these birds until they are 6 to 8 months old -- or longer.

Any hatchery that does claim to send female chicks only should also offer a replacement policy for roosters. Generally such a policy reads along these lines, "We offer a one-time replacement policy for roosters at no charge over shipping. This guarantee expires 6 months after the date of purchase. Replacement chicks will be the same age or younger than those in the original order, and may or may not be the same color depending on current stock."

A typical cost for Silkie chicks is $3.50 (£2.31) per chick. The price tends to go down as the number of chicks in the order goes up.

When you buy live chickens online, the birds will be sent by some means of express mail. Typically boxes hold from 1 to 6 chicks, but few reputable breeders will ship a chick alone, especially in a breed as sociable as the Silkie.

You need to time the shipping arrival for a weekday so the birds can be picked up as soon as possible at the post office. If the chicks are to be delivered to your home, it is crucial that someone be there when the box is delivered, and that the chicks are removed and looked after as soon as possible.

4. How to Tell if Chicks Are Healthy

When you buy Silkie chicks in person, make sure they appear healthy, bright eyed, and alert. Gently pick up the chick and examine its backside, which should be fluffy and clean. If you find a wet, sticky mess, don't buy the chick. It may have been kept in damp conditions and could be sick from being chilled or it may not have been fed properly and is suffering from gastrointestinal distress. Even if another chick in the same bunch looks fine, beware. Poultry diseases in chicks are highly contagious and generally fatal.

Be sure not to select a bird that is holding its feathers fluffed out or its wings out and away from its body. This could be a sign of nutritional deficiency. When chicks don't get enough protein in their diet, they're droopy and slow to grow out their feathers. Any evidence of blood in the droppings is a sign of coccidiosis.

5. Precautions About Hatchery Chicks

Silkies for sale from hatcheries are generally of a lower quality, and are much more likely to have malformed feet. This is a consequence of the flock being poorly managed. Only chickens that are in perfect health and that are fed the correct diet will produce high-quality eggs. If you are looking for a show-quality Silkie, you are much better off going to a breeder.

While inbreeding is common among show birds, it's much easier to assess the quality of a breeder's chickens from their successful record in the ring, and from their physical appearance. Most breeders will sell pet-quality Silkie bantam chickens for sale at a greatly reduced rate because they love the birds and want to see them go to a good home. If you want a show-quality bird, you may have to wait 4-6 months before the breeder is willing to release the chicks.

Chapter 5 - Daily Care of Silkie Chickens

Silkie chicken care on a daily basis means providing food and water at all times and ensuring they live in a well-maintained environment. Grooming and maintenance may involve dusting your chickens to keep them free of parasites, bathing the bird, or even trimming its beak and toenails.

The wonderful thing about Silkies, however, is that they will willingly cooperate with pretty much anything you need to do for and with them. They are wonderfully docile creatures, and actually enjoy the interaction. Surprisingly, these delightful pets are so receptive to bathing, some owners say their birds doze off during the process!

1. Food and Water, Availability and Containers

Food and water should be available to your chickens at all times.

A typical design for a feeder that holds commercial mixes is a central receptacle that sits in a tray or lid with individual feeding compartments. The lid screws off to allow the receptacle to be filled. When the lid is back in place, the feeder is turned right side up and the force of gravity draws the grain into the compartments. Expect to pay $20 to $30 (£13.08 to £19.77) for one of these units. They are available in plastic and metal.

The same style is used for chicken water dispensers, which are available in the same price range. Some people use "ball" or "nipple" water dispensers, which are similar to those used with rabbits and Guinea pigs. Chickens need clean, fresh water at all times, so go with what your chicken will use and what you can most easily keep filled.

When used in a coop or yard, elevate the containers to the height of the chicken's back to prevent feces and litter from being scratched into the container. Chickens are foraging omnivores.

They spend their days scratching and pecking for food, so their feed container should be filled at all times, and fresh, clean water should always be available.

Contamination from scratching is less of an issue with house chickens. Just ensure that the bird has free access to both food and water throughout the day.

Store your chicken's food in metal containers so it does not become damp or attract mice, rodents, and insects. Throw away any food that has become moldy or that shows any sign of parasite activity.

2. Types of Foods for Your Chickens

The choice of food for your Silkie chicken will be dependent on the age of the bird.

If you have hatched chicks that have NOT been vaccinated against coccidiosis (see Chapter 6 - Overview of Silkie Chicken Health for more details) you will want to choose a medicated starter feed.

If your chicks HAVE been vaccinated, you want a non-medicated feed. *This is extremely important.* If you use a medicated feed with chicks that have been vaccinated for coccidiosis, the feed will cancel out the effect of the vaccination.

Starter Feeds

You want your starter mixture to be 18-20% protein. There are many starter chicken feeds available on the market, some costing under $25 (£16.48) for 50 lb. (22.67 kg) sacks.

A typical product like Manna Pro Chick Starter Feed is offered in 5 lb. (2.26 kg) bags for approximately $6.95 (£4.58). This is a medicated feed intended as the sole feed for chicks from 0 to 8 weeks. It is a mixture of grain and plant products with copper supplementation, so it should not be fed to any copper-sensitive species like sheep.

Growing and Finishing Feeds

After 18 weeks, most people switch to a "growing and finishing" nutrition product like Purina Flock Raiser SunFresh Recipe. It is made of plant-based ingredients and is free of any animal proteins and fats. The mixture is available in both pellet and crumble format. Since Silkies are small birds, they tend to do better with crumbles. Keep your birds on this mix through week 22 of life.

A 5 lb. (2.26 kg) sack of Flock Raiser sells for approximately $5 (£3.30).

Adult Feeds

Adult chickens need 16-18% protein for life. Although Silkies are not great laying chickens, producing only about 3 eggs a week, it's perfectly alright to feed them a standard laying mix like Purina Layena, which also comes in the SunFresh Recipe as both pellets and crumbles in the same price range ($5 (£3.30) per 5 lb. (2.26 kg) sack.)

Note: If your chickens don't like any of the mainstream products mentioned, there are many commercial feeds available. Just pay attention to the age appropriateness of the product and the protein content.

Grit

Additionally, your birds need grit, which is a mixture of limestone and granite. This helps them to digest their food. Check the labels, but commercial foods should already contain grit. If your birds are allowed to peck and scratch outside, they will pick up small rocks on their own.

Beware of any swelling on the chest, however, that indicates that their crop could be blocked. (The crop is a muscular pouch adjacent to the esophagus where grit is stored for the purpose of softening the bird's food before it passes to the stomach and digestive system.)

Treats for Your Silkies

One of the easiest aspects of keeping Silkies is that they'll eat almost anything, so it's very simple to augment their diet with treats straight out of your own kitchen. Some particularly good treats for your chickens include:

- Bananas (peeled) are an excellent source of potassium.
- Berries of all kinds. (If you feed your chickens strawberries, wash them well since this is a heavily sprayed fruit.)
- Grapes are great fun because the chickens not only like them, but tend to play with them.
- Lettuce and kale are terrific, but avoid iceberg lettuce simply because it has little food value.
- Melons, pumpkins and squash with the seeds. (Your chickens will like them.)
- Cooked pasta or macaroni is a real favorite.
- Cooked oatmeal.
- Popped popcorn without salt and butter.
- Sunflower seeds.
- Plain yogurt.

Give your chickens bread in moderation only. They don't need a lot of starch, but if you have trimmed crusts, or part of a loaf that has gone stale, that's fine.

Also, you can buy live crickets and mealworms at the pet store and watch your Silkies go to town doing what they do best, hunting insects!

Clean up quickly after giving your chickens any of these treats, since you don't want any decomposing scraps left in their enclosure.

*A **Special Note on Feed:*** In the United States, the southern and western states have suffered severe drought conditions that began late in 2011 and continued into 2012. As a result of its weakened condition, the surviving corn crop has been heavily contaminated with alphatoxins and mycotoxins, which are extremely dangerous for poultry. Commercial feeds usually include toxin binders to eliminate problems with these contaminants, but it's important to check labels. Some Silkie chicken owners grind their own grains for food. If so, toxin binders purchased at your local feed store should be added to the mixture.

3. Cleaning the Enclosure

There is no better safeguard for your chicken's health than daily and thorough cleaning of its enclosure and coop. Silkie chickens are especially susceptible to problems with their feet, since parasites love to burrow into their feathered shanks and toes. Don't let dirt or soiled bedding accumulate on the floor of their enclosure. This material will crust under their toenails and form a breeding ground for microscopic organisms and the diseases they cause.

A chicken's enclosure should be well-ventilated, with no areas where moisture can accumulate. Remove soiled bedding and droppings daily, and make sure the chicken has a place to roost off the ground at night. Treat outdoor enclosures monthly against parasites including mites and lice. Choose either diatomaceous earth, which is non-toxic, or an agricultural insecticide powder like Sevin dust.

4. Seasonal Care

Silkie chickens do remarkably well during the cold months, but they are highly susceptible to heat. If you live in an area where daily temperatures rise into the high 90s F (32.2 C) or above, make sure that your birds have plenty of fresh, cool water and consider adding a mister and a fan to their enclosure. Some breeders air condition coops that house show chickens.

Obviously this is not a concern for house chickens, but do be aware that all birds are prone to respiratory disease, and should not be left in a drafty space or allowed to catch a chill.

5. Monitoring Your Chickens' Health

A major advantage of monitoring a Silkie chicken's health is the breed's great receptivity to being handled. Simply touching and interacting with your chicken daily will give you a much better chance of spotting any health issues in their very early stages.

You will always see a greater problem with mites and lice in the warmer months. Birds that have the opportunity to take dust baths, or those that are bathed regularly should not experience major issues with parasites, but it's still a good idea to treat the pens and coop with diatomaceous earth or an insecticide power during the spring and summer.

This is also the time of year that you will want to be especially vigilant to examine your chicken's feathered legs for any sign of scaly leg mites, which can cause itching, swelling, and bleeding. (See Chapter 6 - Overview of Silkie Chicken Health for a complete description of this problem.)

Watch your bird's overall behavior. Any signs of lethargy, diminished appetite, unexplained feather loss, or discharge from the eyes or nose should be evaluated immediately. Keep feces out of the food and water dishes, and clean the enclosure and coop daily. Do not let dampness build up, as that is where many dangerous organisms thrive.

Any sign of blood in the feces or urine is a sure sign of illness, likely Coccidiosis, which can prove fatal in just six days. (See Chapter 6 for a more complete discussion of this and other common chicken diseases.)

6. Maintenance and Grooming

The primary grooming needs you will need to fulfill for your chicken involve beak and toenail trimming. The latter is especially important as Silkies have a fifth toe. Bathing is not necessary in pets, but is essential in show birds. Also expect to have to keep the bird's fluffy crest in shape, either to ensure that it's clean for showing, or so the bird can see where it's going!

Filing Your Chicken's Beak

Chickens that have access to the outdoors will rub their beaks against rocks and rough surfaces to keep them trimmed and ground into shape. House chickens may need your help with this task.

In most cases a good quality nail file or a very fine carving file is sufficient to simply shorten and reshape the beak. Be careful not to get carried away, however. The beak is a highly vascular organ and will bleed.

If you've ever clipped a dog or cat's claws and hit the "quick" you'll understand that it not only hurts the animal, but can result in a frightening amount of blood. For this reason, many people who keep house chickens prefer to seek help from their vet when it's time to file their pet's beak.

Trimming Your Chicken's Toenails

Silkies are unique in the poultry world not only for their downy soft feathers, but also for their fifth toe, which rarely touches the ground. Chickens who are outside scratching take care of their own pedicures, but even outdoor Silkies may need that fifth toenail clipped. If the nail gets too long, the bird won't be able to walk properly. If you have a rooster, his spurs will need trimming as well.

Just like any animal with toenails, a chicken's nail has a vascular "quick" that will bleed. Always trim in front of the quick. Use clippers designed for a dog, or a very strong pair of human nail clippers. If you cannot see the quick on darker nails, look at the nail from the underside, or use a flashlight pressed against the nail. Always trim conservatively.

If you're concerned about catching the quick, trim a little off the nail every couple of weeks. Silkies are very docile birds. They enjoy being handled and will quickly get used to the whole business.

Bathing Your Chicken

Silkies are incredibly cooperative about being bathed. This is certainly a necessary process for show chickens, but it can be a pleasurable one for family pets as well. Bathing will also aid in removing mites while conditioning the bird's skin and keeping it clear of any contaminants.

To bathe your chicken you will need two tubs of water that are deep enough for the bird to be submerged up to its neck.

The water should be pleasantly warm, but not hot.

Use a mild shampoo. One that is designed for puppies or kittens is fine, but any "no tears" formula will work. Additionally, have some white vinegar on hand.

Set aside 1 or 2 towels, a hair dryer, a soft toothbrush, and unscented petroleum jelly.

Add a small amount of shampoo to the first tub and mix until a nice froth of bubbles forms. Gently place your Silkie in the bath and massage the warm soapy water into the feathers, working with the direction of their growth. Pay special attention to the area under the wings and around the vent.

Use the toothbrush to gently scrub the legs and under the toenails.

The second tub should be filled with warm, clean water. Add a little bit of vinegar, which removes oil and residue from the feathers.

Gently place the chicken in the tub and pour clean warm water over the bird, avoiding the head, until all traces of shampoo are gone. If necessary, change out the rinse water for a fresh batch. Be careful not to allow the bird to get chilled.

When the chicken's feathers have been thoroughly rinsed, wrap the bird in a towel and pat as much water out of the feathers as you can. By this point, your Silkie may well be so relaxed it will be half asleep!

When the bird has been dried as much as possible with the towel, use the blow dryer on the lowest setting to finish drying the feathers and fluff them out. You will be surprised to discover that Silkies don't mind the sound of the hairdryer in the slightest, and very much enjoy the warm air and the petting motion.

When the bird is completely dry, lightly coat the feet and nails with the petroleum jelly as a moisturizer, and as a protection against parasites like scaly leg mites.

While the grooming of show chickens can be even more involved, and extend to keeping their crests carefully pinned back with styling tape, any pet chicken will benefit from and enjoy the attention of a day at the "spa."

Caring for Your Silkie Chicken's Crest

As mentioned above, people who show Silkies will often tie or tape their crests back so the feathers do not become stained. Once white feathers are discolored, it's very hard to get them pristine again. Over and above this problem, however, your Silkie's crest may well interfere with the bird's ability to see! If that's the case, hold the bird in your lap, and very gently and slowly trim the long ends of the crest back. You will not hurt the bird by clipping its feathers.

7. Managing Stress in the Environment

Often when chickens fall into ill health, they are reacting to stress in their environment. Signs of stress include feather picking, vent pecking, and egg eating. For most breeds, excessive handling is the number one stressor. Thankfully, this is NOT the case with Silkie chickens. These birds are the friendliest of all breeds and actually thrive on interaction with humans. They are loyal and affectionate to the point of following their people around to see what's going on. Silkies are more likely to be stressed by things like:

- The sudden introduction of new chickens into the environment.
- Insufficient food and water.
- Extreme heat.
- Egg laying.
- The presence of other animals that pester them.
- Overcrowded conditions.

Birds that have an adequate amount of space, that are fed a well-balanced diet, and that live in clean, well-maintained cages are generally happy and stress free. As a rule of thumb, introduce your Silkie chicken to new experiences slowly. Learn your bird's personality, and don't go beyond its tolerance levels for things like noise, sudden movements, or the presence of other animals.

Silkies are docile, cooperative animals and make wonderful pets, just remain sensitive to your chicken's needs. The bird can't talk, but if it begins to display signs of distress and agitation, the message is still crystal clear. Something is going on that is stressing the animal. Left unaddressed, high levels of stress can cause death in chickens, so be attentive to your bird's reactions to the world around it and act accordingly.

8. Approximate Monthly Costs

The cost of keeping chickens is surprisingly minimal after the initial investment in an enclosure and coop for the birds. Even sacks of grain and feed that weigh as much as 50 lbs. (22.68 kg) cost under $25 (£16.48).

- A 50 lb. (22.68 kg) sack of Purina scratch grains, which is a feed supplement for adult chickens costs approximately $23 (£15.16).
- The "Start & Grow" Recipe by the same manufacturer averages $22 (£14.50) for 50 lbs. (22.68 kg)
- The Flock Raiser Sun Fresh Crumble mix is $22 (£14.50) for 50 lbs. (22.68 kg)

If you have only 3 or 4 chickens, any of these products, stored well, will last you 3 to 4 months. Since chickens are omnivores, their diet can be augmented with table scraps, and they will also eat — and enjoy — insects.

Previously discussed one-time expenses might include:

- A diaper cover for indoor chickens $25 - $30 (£16.48 - £19.77).
- A harness and leash $12 - $20 (£7.91 - £13.18)

Silkies can easily be transported in the same kind of travel crates used for dogs and cats, which average $25 to $50 (£16.48 to £32.96)

While coops and enclosures can range from $200 to $2000 (£131.83 to £1318.30) depending on size and complexity, chicken feeders and waterers can be purchased for approximately $20 (£13.18) each.

Taking the enclosure expense out of the equation, initial equipment costs are just $100 to $150 (£65.92 to £98.87)

Chapter 6 - Overview of Silkie Chicken Health

The more familiar you are with your Silkie and its personality, the easier it will be for you to monitor your pet's health and detect potential illnesses.

1. Warning Signs of Illness

Pay attention to your chicken's eyes. Don't just look for signs of discharge, but look for that bright-eyed, curious gaze that is a hallmark of the Silkie breed. When a chicken's eyes are dull and listless, and the animal does not seem alert and interested, something is likely to be wrong. Other factors to consider include:

- Condition of the feathers, especially the tail feathers. Drooping tail feathers are a warning signal.

- Appetite and thirst. Is the bird eating and drinking normally?

- Does the tail bob up and down as the bird breathes? If so, the animal is in respiratory distress.

- What is the color of the comb and wattles? Are they pale or blotchy?

- Are there any lumps or physical abnormalities on the body? If this occurs in the chest, the crop could be blocked.

- Is there any discharge from the eyes or nose?

- Is the bird pecking at itself or plucking its own feathers?

- Is the bird molting at the wrong time of year?

- Is the chicken being pecked by the other birds? A sick chicken can literally be pecked to death by others of its own kind.

Any change in behavior, attitude, and appetite is a cause for concern, and should be evaluated.

Whole books have been written about diseases common to poultry. The conditions you are most likely to encounter with your Silkies are coccidiosis, mite and lice infestations, scaly leg mite, Marek's, water on the brain, mycoplasma, and salmonella.

2. Coccidiosis

Coccidiosis is the most common and costly of all diseases in chickens. In large poultry farms, approximately 10 to 20 birds out of every 100 will be affected by these microscopic protozoan parasites, which are present in the chickens' droppings. Because the birds are very messy, especially when they are scratching, both their food and water can become contaminated. When a chicken swallows feces, the coccidia invade the intestines and begin to grow.

Infection can occur at any age, but chicks aged 4 to 8 weeks are at the greatest risk, which is why many hatcheries and breeders vaccinate chicks against coccidiosis or use medicated feed. (Note that you cannot do both. If your chicks have been vaccinated, medicated feed will cancel out the effect of the vaccination.)

Coccidiosis runs its course in 6 days, but there are no apparent symptoms until day 3 or 4 when the bird will become listless, stop eating, and begin ruffling its feathers for no apparent reason. The greatest numbers of deaths occur on the fifth day, when blood appears in the droppings and the bird is in acute physical distress. If the chicken lives to the sixth day, it will pass the growths in its intestines and will likely survive.

In addition to vaccinating young birds or using medicated feeds, it's crucial to keep both food and water sources clear of droppings. Do not overcrowd the chicken enclosure, which should be well maintained with dry litter and good cross ventilation.

3. Mites and Lice

Chickens, like all birds, are prone to infestations of mites and lice, especially if they are housed outdoors. Every couple of weeks, look under the wings and around the vent for clusters of parasite eggs at the base of the feathers. If chickens are infested with red mites that are nocturnal, the birds will stamp on their roosts in reaction to the irritation. Scaling on the face, comb, and wattles indicates the presence of the Northern fowl mite.

When mites or lice are present, the whole coop must be thoroughly cleaned and dusted, and the bird must be dusted as well, with a second treatment 10 days later. The commercial insecticide Sevin dust has long been considered a standard for treating both the coop and the bird, however, the product has been linked to declining honey bee populations, and there is concern about the chemicals it contains leaching into the bird's flesh.

A second option is cat or dog flea powder, which will contain permethrine, but it is also a potential toxin, which can leach into eggs. Adverse effects from the use of commercial flea powders with dogs and cats make many chicken owners reluctant to use the powder.

The current treatment of choice, although slower acting than chemical agents is diatomaceous earth, a fine granite powder that cuts into the parasites' exoskeleton and kills them. It is perfectly safe to use on the birds and has no toxic properties.

4. Scaly Leg Mite

This microscopic mite (Cnemidocoptes mutans) is common in Silkie chickens due to their feathered legs. The parasite burrows under the scales on the chicken's leg causing them to become raised. Skin cells and the mite's excrement create an itchy, white crust resembling salt. The legs will bleed and appear swollen, causing discomfort for the bird and impairing its ability to walk. If left unattended, blood circulation in the leg is affected. The foot may become deformed, and toes may have to be removed.

The recommended treatment is to use common petroleum jelly from the drug store to soften the crust. Use baby oil to soothe the itching and make the chicken more comfortable. After a week, hold the chicken's legs in a warm, soapy bath. A pet shampoo or any "no tears" human formula will work.

Use a soft toothbrush to gently loosen the crusty deposits and remove them. Stop if the legs begin to bleed. After the bath, fill a wide-necked jar with rubbing alcohol. Dunk each of the chicken's legs in the alcohol for 30 seconds. Repeat this entire process once a week for three weeks.

Treat the chickens' house with a designated poultry mite powder, and lightly coat the birds' perches with vegetable oil. Mites thrive in damp conditions. Make sure the chicken coop is well ventilated and remove any collections of damp bedding, being careful not to allow them to accumulate again.

5. Marek's Disease

Marek's Disease is common to the Silkie breed. The disease is caused by a virus in the herpes family that attacks lymph tissue, causing tumor growth and peripheral nerve damage. Typically, one of the wings and one leg will become paralyzed, and the bird may go blind. Often the legs will tremble, and the bird's neck may become twisted (torticollis.) Other symptoms include increased molting, a drop in egg production, and disoriented behavior.

The infection occurs when the bird inhales feather debris or "dander" containing the virus. Since it is airborne, the virus can be spread at a considerable distance from an infected flock on adjoining property.

Once in the bird's system, the virus takes hold quickly and then lies dormant for one to six months until symptoms appear in response to some stressing agent. Hens infected with the virus, for instance, can begin to show symptoms after laying eggs.

Antibiotics can ease some of the chicken's symptoms, but death is a likely result of Marek's Disease. Those birds that do live become carriers of the virus, which is so contagious that culling of the affected birds to save the others in the flock is the best solution.

Silkie chickens should be vaccinated subcutaneously (under the skin) against Marek's Disease when they are a day old, with a "booster" in two weeks. Younger birds should be kept away from older chickens until they are 5 months of age to allow their natural resistance to develop. Marek's is seen less often in colder climates.

6. Water on the Brain

High-quality Silkie chickens have domed skulls that enhance their feathered crests. In chicks, this dome looks like a large bump on top of the head, and is often mistaken by new owners as a congenital deformity, or even a tumor. This enlargement of the cranial cavity can produce excess fluid, which presses on the brain.

Symptoms of "water on the brain" include walking backwards, and falling over for no apparent reason. Many birds spin in circles, and then stop abruptly.

Birds exhibiting this kind of behavior should be isolated and fed a liquid diet of pellets ground in water through a syringe every two to four hours during the day. The chicken will need an antibiotic and an anti-inflammatory injection administered by a veterinarian.

The treatment period can last as long as a month before the swelling goes down, but in severe cases, the bird may have to be euthanized.

7. Mycoplasma

This is a common and highly infectious respiratory disease that requires weeks of antibiotic treatment. It is difficult to eradicate in a flock, and incidents of recurrence are high. The classic signs include puffy eyes, discharge from the eyes and nose, and sneezing.

Because the bird's sinuses are full, the chicken becomes lethargic and will often stop eating. Dehydration is a serious danger, and is evident if the skin of the wattles becomes paler than usual. The disease is often difficult to spot until the birds are too weak to be saved.

8. Taking Precautions Against Salmonella Infection from Live Chickens

It is possible for Salmonella germs to be present in chicken feces as well as on their bodies, even when the chickens are clean and well looked after. Salmonella lives naturally in the intestines of many types of poultry and can make humans sick with abdominal cramps, diarrhea, vomiting and fever. Infants, young children and the elderly or anyone with a weakened immune system can be susceptible to such an infection. If Salmonella poisoning spreads to the bloodstream, it can result in death if not promptly treated with antibiotics.

People can become infected with Salmonella when they have handled anything that has come into contact with the germs and then touch the area in or around their mouths. The following precautions, as outlined by the U.S. Centers for Disease Control, will help to lessen your chance of picking up Salmonella germs from your Silkies.

- After handling live poultry or anything in the area where the birds live or roam, wash your hands thoroughly with soap and water. If soap and water are not available, use a high quality hand sanitizer.

- Do not let young children under the age of 5 handle chickens without supervision.

- Don't eat or drink in the area where your chickens live or where they are free to roam.

- If you collect eggs from your chickens, cook the eggs thoroughly. Salmonella germs can pass from the hen to the interior of their eggs.

- Do not allow poultry into areas where food is being prepared or consumed.

It's always better to assume that Salmonella is present than to ignore the risk. The best safeguard against accidental contamination is to thoroughly clean the chickens' enclosure and all equipment used with them regularly.

9. Finding Poultry Veterinarians

In rural areas it will not be difficult to find a veterinarian to advise you on monitoring your chickens' health and treating problems. Many chicken owners take it upon themselves to learn about chicken diseases and to tackle treatment procedures on their own since many remedies are well established with proven cure rates.

In urban areas, where vets are more accustomed to treating dogs and cats, it can be more difficult to find someone who will take care of a pet chicken. Owners can contact The American College of Poultry Veterinarians at www.acpv.info or the World Veterinary Poultry Association at www.wpva.net to locate veterinarians in their area.

Since items like lice and mite powders and many antibiotics can be purchased online from poultry and feed supply outlets, the cost of healthcare for your chicken should be minimal unless office visits to a vet are required.

For example, a 10-ounce bag of Amprol, an antibiotic used for the treatment of coccidiosis, typically costs $25 online before shipping. Bacitracin, used to treat gastrointestinal issues in chicks, costs around $28.

Chapter 7 - Breeding and Raising Silkie Chickens

Silkie chickens are one of those pets that lead their owners to want more, or to have the experience of raising a Silkie from birth. The decision to breed and raise Silkies is largely dependent on available space, whether you're letting the hen do all the work or whether you decide to hatch fertilized eggs on your own in an incubator. The latter decision means buying equipment and making a two-month commitment to hatching and brooding care.

1. Natural Hatching v. Incubators

Obviously Silkie hens, with their superb maternal instincts, have the best qualifications to be raising young of their own kind. If you have the room to let one of your hens raise babies, go for it! She'll love the experience and so will you. There are, however, some compelling reasons to hatch chicks out from the fertilized eggs you've purchased.

If you have young children and part of your motivation for having chickens is for the educational value of the total experience, then starting from "scratch" is the way to go. If this is the case, you need to understand exactly what you're getting into before you place your order for Silkie chicken eggs.

2. Choosing an Incubator

There is no factor more important in hatching chickens in an incubator than temperature regulation. Do not buy an incubator without a fan and a thermometer that can be calibrated. Also, get a unit that is easy to clean. If you plan on hatching more than one set of eggs, the incubator must be thoroughly cleaned and sanitized. Eggshells are highly porous and easily contaminated with germs.

After temperature, humidity is the next most critical environmental factor. The incubator will be outfitted with water trays, which you will need to refill and maintain according to the manufacturer's instructions. It is recommended that an incubator be allowed to run at least a week before the eggs are placed inside to allow the unit's internal environment to stabilize.

If you have chosen a well-made incubator, and if the fertilized eggs you purchased are top quality, expect a successful hatching rate of 50-85 percent.

Pricing an Incubator

Incubators come in two primary styles: tabletop and cabinet. Capacities range from units that will hold 40-60 eggs to those large enough for 120-140. As a general rule of thumb, the cabinet models hold the largest number of eggs.

Using IncubatorWarehouse.com as a source for pricing, the Little Giant Egg Incubator for $67.50 (£44.49) is a good example of a unit that would be acceptable for a small number of eggs. It has a capacity for up to 46 eggs, includes an electronic thermostat, built-in humidity control, a bulb thermometer, and the option for a circulated air fan.

The fact that there are two large viewing windows makes this an ideal unit for use with children curious to know what's going on with the whole process! (This company will ship internationally with a three-day order fulfillment period.)

This price range is a good starting point to compare any incubator units you are considering. Read all relevant customer reviews, and make certain the unit has the necessary features to properly maintain the environment throughout the incubation unit. Some people prefer incubators with automatic egg turners, but be prepared to pay more.

3. Incubation and Hatching

From the time you place the fertilized eggs in the incubator until the chicks hatch, you're looking at 19 to 21 days.

The temperature inside the incubator should be set at 99.5 to 100 degrees F (37.5 to 37.7 C) for a forced air unit and 101 to 102 degrees F (38.3 to 38.8 C) for still air.

For the first 18 days, little water will be added to the incubator since the required humidity is only about 20 percent. It's best to lightly mist the eggs every couple of days. On Day 18, the humidity should be increased to 65 percent.

Some incubators have automatic turners to rotate the eggs. If not, you will need to turn them by hand several times a day through the first 18 days, at which time the chicks begin to get into the proper position for hatching.

Between Day 19 and Day 21 you will hear the chicks making sounds. Do not open the incubator once the chicks are audible. Releasing the humidity in the unit could cause the babies to get stuck inside their shells.

Once the chicks have hatched, allow them to remain in the incubator for 24 hours before moving them to the brooder for the purpose of further protecting the chicks.

A brooder can be something as simple as a cardboard box under a heating lamp. The main thing to understand is that because the chicks are only covered in down, and have no adult feathers, they cannot maintain their own body temperature. They will need "mothering" in a contained environment during the first month of their lives if they are to survive.

4. Brooding Newly Hatched Chicks

When you choose to raise chicks from fertilized eggs, or you purchase newly hatched chicks, you are, in essence, becoming a surrogate mother.

The brooder that you set up and maintain artificially performs the functions a mother hen would undertake to:

- protect her babies from harm
- keep them warm
- guard them against predators
- teach them to eat and drink

Newly hatched chicks cannot take care of themselves. In addition to the 19-21 days spent tending the eggs in the incubator, you are then looking at an additional month brooding.

The chicks must have their feathers grown in before they can be released with other chickens or into a coop or run on their own.

Cost of a Brooder

Since a brooder can be a "do-it-yourself" arrangement, costs will vary widely. You might not have to spend more than $20 (£13.18) to get a 250-watt brooder lamp and bulb. This is not to say, however, that you cannot purchase complete brooder kits.

Using ChickenCoopMart.com as a source for pricing, a chick brooder starter kit that includes an 18" (45.72 cm) high cardboard "corral," a brooder lamp with a dimmer, a hanging clamp, a 100 watt infrared bulb, a one-quart water container, and a feeder is priced at $54.39 (£35.85).

(Please note that this company will only ship inside the United States. This package, however, is a good point of comparison if you are shopping for a complete brooder kit as an all-in-one solution.)

Setting Up Your Brooder

A brooder does not have to be an elaborate, commercially purchased unit. You can use a sturdy box, or even block off an unused corner of a storage room. The area does need to be well ventilated, but you don't want the chicks subjected to any direct drafts at floor level.

You're looking for the perfect mix between air movement to keep the area dry, and adequate warmth. If necessary, draft shields can be used at floor level. You can use simple strips of cardboard for this purpose.

Including a Heat Source

As a heat source, suspend an electric heating element or heat lamp over the area. Ideally, either device will have a means of regulating the output up and down. If you opt for a heat lamp, use two just in case one burns out. Some people use infrared light over clear light, but both seem to work equally well. Take care that your lamp is not near anything that could catch fire and that there is no danger of any water getting on the cord or near the electrical outlet.

Protecting the Chicks from Predators and Over-Handling

At this stage of the chicks' lives, rats can also be a danger to them, so if you have your brooder in a store room, make sure there's no rodent activity in the area and that snakes cannot get in either. Obviously if there's a family cat, the brooding area is strictly off limits.

If there are young children in the household, they will understandably be excited about the baby chicks and want to interact with them. Excessive handling of young chicks is a significant stress, so teach your children to watch and participate in the care of the babies, but to respect how young and fragile they are.

Teaching the Chicks to Drink

Since you are serving as a surrogate mother by brooding the chicks, you will have to take over their early life lessons. The first and most important is teaching them to drink water. Make sure the water is slightly warm and mixed with a poultry electrolyte mix.

Put the water out in a flat dish -- even a jar lid will do. The chicks are born with an instinct to peck. They just need your help to discover water. (After 24 hours the electrolyte mix will no longer be necessary.)

Do not use any waterer after the initial drinking lessons that will allow the chicks to splash or get wet. They chill easily. Set the waterer up on thin blocks so it's about shoulder height for the babies.

Teaching the Chicks to Eat

Get the chicks started eating by scattering age appropriate starter feed on a layer of newspaper or a burlap bag spread on the floor so the chicks can see what they're eating. Their instinct, again, is to look on the "ground." Once they get the taste of their feed, the battle is won and you can begin to use a regular feeder. Chickens "graze" all day, so food should be available to them at all times.

Types of Food

You will give your chicks a "starter feed" for the first four weeks, then progress to a "grower" feed for the next 16 weeks of their lives. If you have had your chickens vaccinated against coccidiosis or Marek's Disease, make sure that you do NOT buy a medicated feed.

(See Chapter 6 - Overview of Silkie Chicken Health for more information on diseases and vaccination.)

Medicated feeds are specifically formulated to combat coccidiosis and most contain the preventative amprollium. If the chicks have been vaccinated, however, amprollium won't hurt the birds, but it will counteract the vaccine and render it useless.

Adding Grit to Aid with Digestion

Chickens eat tiny pebbles, which they store in their crop, a muscular pouch on the esophagus. The pebbles soften their food, since the birds have no teeth. For baby chicks, provide sand or parakeet or canary gravel sprinkled in with their food.

(Read the label of the commercial starter or growth feed you're using. Most have grit in their ingredients.)

Keeping the Brooder Clean

Clean the brooder daily to make sure droppings do not accumulate and serve as a breeding ground for organisms that thrive in decomposing feces.

For bedding, use pine shavings, not cedar as the latter is toxic to chickens. Straw tends to stay too damp for young chicks.

Don't layer the bedding thickly. If the chicks are cold and bunch up for warmth in dense bedding, they can suffocate themselves.

Regulating the Temperature in the Brooder

Adjust the temperature by observing the behavior of the chicks. If they're running around pecking and scratching, they're happy and warm. If they're huddled under the light, they're cold. Chicks do sleep a lot, so don't worry about that, just be on the watch for any huddling behavior.

Chicks must have all their feathers so they can maintain their body temperature on their own before they can be taken out of the brooder. In cooler seasons, this may take a month, but in summer only three weeks or less.

Sexing Baby Chicks

First, let's get our terminology right. A male chicken under one year of age is called a cockerel; a female in the same age range is referred to as a pullet.

It's extremely difficult to determine the gender of Silkie chickens before age 8 or 9 months. The major indicators of sex are as follows:

Comb - In general the comb is large in males and develops more quickly, although this is not always the case.

Crest - The crest of a Silkie cockerel should have "streamers" in the back to create a look that is more "combed back" than round.

The crest of a pullet, on the other hand, has no streamers and is well-rounded.

Wattles - On a male Silkie, the wattles are rounder and larger on the non-bearded variety. In bearded Silkies of both sexes, the wattles are extremely small to the point of being nonexistent.

Spurs - Leg spurs are completely absent on female Silkies.

Crowing - While the crow is thought to be the exclusive purview of cockerels and roosters, hens do sometimes crow, but this is rare.

Eggs - This is, of course, the definitive test. When a Silkie lays an egg, you have a pullet!

Feathering - Silkie males have longer feathers on the neck (the hackles) and the saddle (the area just in front of the tail.) Additionally, these feathers are more pointed at the tip, and the saddle feathers will lay over the wings slightly.

Tail - In female Silkies, the tails are softer and rounder. In show quality birds, however, the tails of both genders should be perfectly round and wide.

It is not at all unusual for even the most experienced breeders of show Silkies to make a mistake sexing young birds. Even at poultry shows, breeders can be found staring at birds and debating their gender.

People who have been working with Silkies for years say that rather than following any scientific approach to sexing the birds, they simply have a sense at 8-12 weeks and more or less guess.

Fifty percent is considered a pretty good success rate at this gender-based guessing game, and in many instances a bird has to crow or lay an egg before anyone is really sure.

5. Avian DNA Sex Determination

Veterinarians, breeders, and owners can use a non-surgical method to determine gender in a number of avian species including Silkie chickens with an accuracy rate of 99.9 percent.

The test can be run on a blood or feather sample. Both methods return the same level of accuracy, but feather samples sometimes do not contain an adequate number of cells for analysis and must be resubmitted.

(Eggshells can be used for DNA testing if the inner membrane is still present.)

Kits for collecting and submitting the sample to a registered lab cost approximately $25 (£16.48) per bird, with turnaround times of 2-10 days depending on location and the lab used.

6. Determining Quality of the Birds

Don't fall for any claims that the show quality of Silkies can be determined either from the eggs or from the chicks.

If there are obvious birth defects like a deformed foot or a scissor bill that disqualify a Silkie (see Chapter 8 - Showing Silkie Chickens) that's one thing, but positive attributes of a show chicken cannot be judged until at least 6 months of age to a year.

7. Common Birth Defects in Silkie Chickens

In many cases birth defects result in the death of baby chicks. As long as the chick can walk, eat, and drink, loving owners can work around almost any physical issue, but in the end the decision is always one of quality of life.

All too often, the chicks simply die because they do not have the strength and physical means to thrive.

Two of the most common birth defects in Silkie chickens are:

- scissor beak - In this condition the upper and lower portion of the beak are misaligned. Most Silkie chickens born with this condition adapt, but the birds are not of show quality. The only time a bird with scissor beak must be euthanized is if the misalignment impairs the bird's ability to eat and drink.

Chickens naturally trim their beaks by rubbing them against rocks and other hard surfaces. Birds with scissor beaks have a difficult time accomplishing this self-maintenance so that owners may have to use dog clippers or a file to trim the beak.

This must be done with great care, however, as beaks are highly vascular and will bleed heavily if trimmed too far back. Styptic powder can be used to stop the bleeding.

- foot deformities

Silkie chickens, unlike other breeds, should have five toes, but foot deformities are common in this breed.

They may exhibit additional toes (polydactylism) or fewer toes, the toes can curl under, be webbed like a duck, or joined by an excessive degree of tissue to create a club foot of sorts.

Any of these deformities are sufficient to have an otherwise perfect bird disqualified from being shown. (It should be noted that these types of birth defects are very common in birds obtained from hatcheries.)

There are a wide range of birth defects possible in domestic poultry from splayed legs to single combs.

If the Silkie chick survives to adulthood, it is considered a "pet quality" bird, but cannot be shown in competition.

Silkies are so personable and loved by their keepers that a great body of practical knowledge has been amassed online about caring for birds with highly specific physical issues.

If you hatch a chick with a birth defect, it's highly advisable to seek input from other Silkie owners. (See the List of Relevant Websites at the back of this book for more information.)

Chapter 8 - Showing Silkie Chickens

Young people most often show chickens under the auspices of an organization like 4H or the Future Farmers of America. In an organized program of this nature, materials will be provided about breed standards, preparing a bird for show, and the fine points of showmanship. This can be a complicated procedure, which is not the purpose of this book, and is often best taught in a one-on-one setting.

However, to get a sense of what is involved in participating in a poultry show, here is a broad overview of the time leading up to the show and what actually happens in the show ring.

1. Before the Show

Make sure that your Silkie is healthy. Not only will a healthy bird stand a much greater chance in competition, but it will also survive the stress of being at the show surrounded by other chickens and by people.

Additionally, chicken diseases and parasites are highly contagious. Don't expose the other chickens at the show to your bird if it is not in perfect health.

Although everyone has a different protocol for getting their birds ready for judging, a general timeline will include these milestones:

- About 12 weeks before the show, remove any broken feathers to allow adequate time for re-growth. This is less a problem with Silkies given the downy nature of their plumage, but the feathers on their legs and feet should be examined for damage.

- About a month before the show trim your bird's beak, toenails, and/or spurs as necessary. You want the edges to have smoothed back over by the time the bird is exhibited.

- A week before the show, give your Silkie a good bath and pin, tie, or tape back its crest to ensure it stays clean. If your chicken is white, you can use a tiny bit of bluing — just a drop or two — to make the feathers snowier. Be careful! Too much bluing, and you will have a blue bird.

- Three to four days before the show, bathe the bird again. This is especially important in a downy breed like the Silkie because you're going for maximum "poofiness" on the day of the show.

At this stage of the game you must keep the bird's cage absolutely pristine with fresh bedding daily. (Some exhibitors bathe their Silkies the day before a show as well.)

Don't forget to add white vinegar to the rinse water, as this will remove oils and other residue from the feathers.

- The day of the show make sure the Silkie's feet are completely free of dirt and feces. You may want to apply a very thin layer of petroleum jelly to the feet, legs, comb, earlobes, beak, and wattles to enhance their sheen.

At the show, enjoy yourself! This is an opportunity to be with other people who love Silkie chickens as much as you do. You can learn a lot from breeders and other exhibitors. If you are planning on breeding your chicken, a show can also be the poultry equivalent of the dating game where you play match maker for your birds.

2. Silkie Chicken Showmanship

Developing showmanship and rapport with your bird doesn't happen overnight. You will need to practice. Fortunately, Silkies make this very easy since they are so good-natured and cooperative. You will, however, want to practice walking with your Silkie, since you will need to carry it from its cage to the show ring, and you will need to repeatedly place your bird on a table and teach it to stay in place.

This is simply a matter of repetition. Put the bird down. Wait for the bird to start walking away. Pick the bird up and put it down again, rewarding the Silkie every time it stands still. You need to work toward a standing duration of 2 to 3 minutes before you start learning to pose the chicken.

When you pose a Silkie, you have to fluff up the tail, and perk the bird's head by holding a treat in your fingers and slowly moving it upward. The idea is to get the chicken to stretch its neck up and slightly forward.

Next, if the judge requires that you introduce yourself in the ring, practice giving the correct information, which includes:

Your name and age.
Your 4H, FFA, or other organization.
The gender of your bird.*
The bird's age.
The bird's class, breed, and variety.

*For show purposes female birds under six months of age are pullets, those six months or older are hens. Male birds under six months are cockerels, those six months and older are cocks.

Examining the Bird

This is the most difficult part of showmanship, but only because the steps must be done in order. Again — practice with your bird.

Head - Hold the bird's head up on your finger, and look at its eyes, beak, and comb. Do this on both sides of the head. Be prepared for the judge to ask you questions about what you see.

Wings - Fan out the wings by grasping the shoulder joint and very gently pulling the wing outward. Lift the wing up and blow out the feathers underneath. The judge will be looking to see if the bird has any visible signs of parasites.

Under color - Lift the feathers on the saddle and neck to both display the under color and to illustrate the absence of parasites.

Width of the Body - Place your thumb and first finger around the widest part of the chicken's body and let the judge see the measurement.

Breast - Flip the bird over and hold its back close to your chest. Measure the length of the keel (breast bone) using your thumb and first finger. Show this measurement to the judge.

Vent - Lower the bird slightly with the head facing toward you. Part the feathers so the judge can see the vent and check for parasites.

Abdomen - Measure the number of fingers that will fit between the breast and pubic bones, which are on either side of the vent, displaying the measurement to the judge.

Width Between the Pubic Bones - See how many fingers will fit between the bird's pubic bones and show the number to the judge.

Feet and Legs - Turn the chicken with its head facing the judge. Hold out the feet and legs and look them over, checking for dirt, scaly leg, or any other irregularities or signs of disease.

Turn the chicken slowly in a full circle, all the while looking at the legs and feet. This is the final step, so wait patiently for the judge when you have finished.

The judge will point out a cage. Walk over with your bird, facing the judge at all times. Put your bird in the cage, pose the chicken, and shut the door. Put your hands behind your back, and wait until the judge nods or asks that you remove the chicken. When so directed, take the bird out and walk back to the table.

3. Suitability of Silkies for Show

Silkie chickens are the perfect breed to participate in poultry shows, especially for young exhibitors who are just getting used to working with livestock and submitting themselves and their animal to judging. Silkies are docile, quiet, cooperative, and like to please their humans.

This is not to say, however, that adults do not show chickens. There are many venues for exhibiting ornamental breeds from county and state fairs to livestock shows. For more information, contact the American Poultry Association or the Silkie Club of Great Britain.

Afterword

Unlike many poultry species, Silkie chickens are not great egg layers. Getting 120 eggs a year — about 3 a week — is considered a high output for these birds. They are edible, but their meat is blue-black and gamey in taste. Considered a delicacy with healing powers in Eastern cultures, Silkies are very rarely raised for meat in the Western world. Instead, as an ornamental breed, Silkies are valued as show animals and pets.

From their likely origin in the ancient Orient, to their travels to Europe in the 16th century along the famed Silk Route, these small, elegant, and docile birds have garnered a special reputation for their amiable personalities and for their unique plumage. The name "Silkie" is well taken, describing perfectly the fur-like quality of their downy feathers that, lacking interlocking barbicels, can only be described as "fluffy" or "hairy."

In addition to their high quality as show animals, Silkie hens are some of the most broody chickens you'll ever meet. Their instinct to set is so strong, they'll hatch out eggs for other species, mother orphaned animals, and in a pinch, settle down optimistically on a pile of rocks. Even the roosters get in the act, ushering the chicks around the yard and offering them tasty insect morsels.

Although the idea of keeping a "house chicken" is relatively new, no breed could be more suited to living inside than a Silkie. They submit willingly to being diapered, and can be trained to use a harness and leash. They're quiet and clever, catching on to games and tricks, and loving to spend time with their humans.

The purpose of this book has been to provide an overview of the breed along with adequate information to help you prepare to bring a Silkie chicken into your life. One of the great things about Silkies, however, is that if you own them for 20 years, they'll continue to surprise and delight you with new insights and knowledge every step of the way.

One final caution. Remember, these are living animals completely dependent on you for their care. Be sure that a Silkie is right for you and that you can provide the right environment for the Silkie before you bring your new pet home. This extends to researching the laws and zoning ordinances that may apply in your area. Prepare everything first. Get all your supplies together, and have your new bird's enclosure ready. Silkies are highly adaptable birds, but like all chickens they are susceptible to stress, so do everything you can to minimize those issues.

Whether you've decided to purchase a young adult bird, a chick, or even fertilized eggs to be hatched in an incubator, Silkies are fun, fascinating, and loving pets from day one. You'll be amazed at how quickly they become part of the family, even if the idea of a pet chicken never occurred to you before. But that's part of the charm of the Silkie breed. They aren't like other chickens, and as soon as you meet one, you'll understand why.

List of Relevant Websites

American Poultry Association at www.amerpoultryassn.com

American Bantam Association at www.bantamclub.com

American Silkie Bantam Club at
www.americansilkiebantamclub.org

The Silkie Club of Great Britain at www.thesilkieclub.co.uk

General Information

Backyard Poultry at www.backyardpoultry.com

Backyard Chickens at www.backyardchickens.com

Fancy Fowl Poultry Magazine at www.fancyfowl.com

Exhibition Poultry Magazine at www.exhibitionpoultry.net

Poultry Press at www.poultrypress.com

Aviculture Europe at www.aviculture-europe.nl (Text in Dutch
and English.)

Purina Poultry Feed at www.purinapoultry.com

Omlet at www.omlet.us

Enclosure Design

BackyardChickens.com

"How to Build the Ultimate Chicken Coop" at http://www.countryliving.com/outdoor/outdoor-living/ultimate-chicken-coop#slide-1

"Keeping Backyard Poultry" at The Centers for Disease Control htto://www.cdc.gov/features/salmonellapoultry

Health

The Association of Avian Veterinarians at www.aav.org

Chinese Silkie Chicken Care at http://www.zoo-zoom.com/Chinese%20Silky%20Chicken.htm

Chicken Health and Behaviour at http://www.newlandgrange.com/CHICKEN-HEALTH-and-BEHAVIOUR(1660699).htm

Chicken and Poultry Health Problems and Diseases at http://smallfarm.about.com/od/chickens/a/Chicken-And-Poultry-Health-Problems-And-Diseases.htm

The Chicken Vet at www.chickenvet.co.uk

Chicken Health for Dummies Cheat Sheet at http://www.dummies.com/how-to/content/chicken-health-for-dummies-cheat-sheet.html

Supplies

Chickens for Backyards at www.chickensforbackyards.com

My Pet Chicken at www.mypetchicken.com

Purina Poultry Feed at www.purinapoultry.com

Premier 1 at www.premier1supplies.com

Tractor Supply Company at www.tractorsupply.com

Hatcheries and Breeders

Cackle Hatchery at www.cacklehatchery.com

Murray McMurray Hatcher at www.mcmurrayhatchery.com

Seriously Silkie at www.seriouslysilkie.com

Hatchery Creek Farm at
hatcherycreekfarm.webs.com/silkiechickens.htm

Backyard Chickens at www.backyardchickens.com

California Hatchery at www.californiahatchery.com

Frizzled Feathers Farm at www.frizzledfeathersfarm.com

Sundown Silkies at www.sundownsilkies.com

eFowl at www.efowl.com

Huckleberry Farm at www.huckfarm.com

Amber Waves Silkies at www.silkiechickens.co

Cheshire Poultry at www.cheshirepoultry.co.uk

Poultry Keeper at www.poultrykeeper.com

Poultry Suppliers in England at
http://www.poultry.allotment.org.uk/poultry-suppliers/poultry-
suppliers-england.php

Frequently Asked Questions and Silkie Chicken Facts

The text of this book covers just about everything you want to know about Silkie chickens from giving one a bath to building a mobile chicken coop, but if you're in a hurry to get started, here are some frequently asked questions about these adorable little fluff balls and what's involved in keeping them as pets.

Why do Silkies have "poofy" feathers?

The individual fibers of most feathers are held together with tiny little barbs that make the feather rigid, but flexible. Silkie feathers don't have those "barbicels," so the individual strands of the feather fluff out like fur or hair.

What else is unique about the Silkie breed?

They have five toes. Their legs and feet are feathered, and their skin, meat, and bones are a dark blue/black color.

If I have Silkie hens, don't I need a rooster, too?

You only need a rooster if you want to raise chicks. If you're looking for an egg-laying chicken, Silkies aren't your best bet. You'll get about 3 eggs a week, or 120 eggs a year (with or without a rooster.)

Are Silkie hens good mothers?

There's no better mother in the poultry world than a Silkie hen. This characteristic is called "broodiness." If a Silkie hen doesn't have chicks of her own to raise, she'll mother any little orphan animal around. Even Silkie roosters get into the act, spending time with the chicks in the yard and bringing them juicy insects as treats.

Are they "Chinese Silkie chickens" or "bantam Silkie chickens?"

Actually, they're both. You'll also see them referred to as a Japanese chicken. "Silky" is an alternate spelling, and they're referred to as bantams. Why all the confusion? These white fluffy chickens originated in Asia and are referred to as Chinese and Japanese chickens. In the United States, they're regarded as bantams. And "Silky" is just a common misspelling. The proper name is "Silkie."

Eight to 15 years is a common lifespan for a chicken. Silkies are smaller birds, do they die sooner?

Not necessarily. A Silkie's lifespan is typically 9 to 10 years, but it's only recently that people have started keeping pet chickens, including house chickens. With good care, it's entirely possible that one of these birds could live as long as 20 years.

At what age do baby Silkies get old enough to start laying eggs?

Typically a hen will start to lay eggs at 5 to 6 months of age, but it may take a Silkie until 8-9 months. Before then, it's almost impossible to determine a Silkie's gender. Sometimes that first egg is the only way you'll know you actually do have a hen!

I see ads for "blue silkie chicken" and "white silkie chicken." How many colors are there?

Silkie chickens come in black, blue, bluff, white, partridge, splash, gray, lavender, red, porcelain, and cuckoo.

How much food will I need for my Silkies? Chickens eat anything, right?

Chickens are omnivores, and they need access to fresh food and water at all times. Typically a hen will eat about 4-6 ounces of feed a day in colder weather, and a bit less in summer. Their consumption also depends on how much access they have to things like table scraps and insects.

I saw an ad online for "silkie chicken for sale" and ordered chicks. They're coming in the mail. How long can they live without food?

Most hatcheries actually send out chicks when they are a day old because right before chicks hatch, they take in all the nutrients in the egg, which are very rich in food value. Typically, newly hatched chicks aren't fed for 2 to 3 days, which is just long enough to get them delivered by express mail, just make sure someone is there to receive the box, and offer the chicks food and water immediately.

I'm interested, but I don't know where to buy silkie chickens?

In many cases the answer is as near as your favorite search engine. Use phrases like "silkie chicken," "silkie chickens for sale," "silky chicken for sale," or "silky chickens for sale." You'll find many listings for hatcheries that will ship eggs and newly hatched chicks. If you're interested in a specific type of Silkie, just alter your search phrase to something like "white silkie chickens for sale." If you don't want to buy online, contact either the American Silkie Bantam Club or the Silkie Club of Great Britain for a directory of breeders in your area.

Can I housebreak my Silkie chicken?

While there are some people who have claimed they've taught their Silkie to "go" on newspapers spread on the floor, conventional wisdom says, no, you can't housebreak a chicken. You can, however, put a diaper on them. For more information see Chapter 4 - Your Silkie Chicken as Part of the Family.

Can I use a leash with my Silkie?

Absolutely. You'll use a chicken harness rather than a collar. It will have a D-ring on the back in the center between the bird's wings. That's where you attach the leash. "Walking" is actually more a matter of you following the chicken around while it pecks and scratches, but the arrangement still puts you in charge of the situation.

Will predators hurt my chickens?

Yes, a range of predators are dangerous to your chickens including raccoons, coyotes, foxes, weasels, skunks, hawks, owls, opossums, bobcats, snakes, squirrels, and domestic cats and dogs.

When can newly hatched chicks join the outside flock?

Don't put chicks outside until they have become fully feathered, usually after a month. They can't regulate their body temperature until their feathers have grown in.

How much room does one chicken need in a coop?

The recommended space for a single chicken in a coop or yard is 4 sq. ft. (0.37m2).

What is the best material to spread on the floor of the coop?

Pine shavings are a good choice. (Don't use cedar as it's toxic to chickens.) Straw is fine, but it must not be allowed to stay damp because it's a natural haven for mites and other parasites, especially when heat builds up.

I saw a listing for a bantam black Silkie chicken. What's the difference between a bantam and a full-sized chicken?

Bantams are generally about a quarter the size of a regular chicken. Silkies average 1.5 − 4 pounds (0.68 − 1.8 kg) in weight.

The website I'm looking at is offering a "straight run" of blue Silkie chickens. What's that?

A straight run is a group of chicks that haven't been sorted by gender. Since it's impossible to tell the sex of the chicks until they're 8-9 months old, the marketer is being honest. You'll likely get all hens, since people who work with these chicks develop a sense about gender over time, but there are no guarantees.

Why aren't my black Silkie chickens laying? Did I get the wrong kind?

There are only two "types" of Silkie, bearded and non-bearded. The colors are just that, colors. No Silkie hen is going to lay a lot of eggs. They just don't. Three a week is considered good production. If you want to raise chickens for the eggs, Silkies aren't the right birds for you.

My buff Silkie chickens are eating their own eggs. What should I do?

It's not just your buffs. Any time chickens start eating their eggs, they likely need more calcium. Buy crushed oyster shells at your local feed store and use it as per directed to supplement their feed.

Can I wash my black Silkie chickens?

Absolutely. All Silkies enjoy a good bath. In Chapter 5 - Daily Care of Silkie Chickens, you'll find a description of how to wash your Silkie and fluff it up afterwards with a blow dryer. They don't mind in the slightest.

What is the best way to introduce new Silkie chickens to my already established flock?

Silkies are really very docile birds, but it's still best to separate the newcomers on the other side of a wire barrier for a couple of weeks. Just let everyone get used to seeing everyone else so there won't be any fighting or aggression. When you do turn them all in together for the first time, be there to supervise so you can break up any incidents.

What happens when a chicken molts?

In the late summer or early fall, chickens lose their feathers and grow them back in. It's a natural process. Your Silkies will look "plucked" for a few weeks, but there's nothing wrong with them.

Do chickens have a particular smell?

No. If there's a bad odor associated with your chickens, their enclosure needs to be cleaned more often.

My daughter wants to show chickens for 4H. Are Silkies a good choice?

Silkies are wonderful chickens for show. They are docile and cooperative, making it much easier for young kids to handle them in the show ring. See the chapter Showing Silkie chickens for a broad overview.

Appendix I - Show Standard in the United States

(*Source*: American Silkie Bantam Club at
http://www.americansilkiebantamclub.org/standard.asp , accessed
May 2013.)

Feather Legged Bantams
Weights: Cock 36 oz. Cockerel 32 oz.
Hen 32 oz. Pullet 28 oz.

Shape - Male and Female

Comb: Male - Walnut - set firmly and evenly on head, almost
circular in shape, preferably broader than longer, with a number
of small prominences over it, a slight indentation or furrow,
transversely across the middle, rising at a point just forward of the
nostrils and extending backwards to a point parallel with the front
of the eyes.
Female - Walnut, very small, well formed. Rest of the description
is the same as the male.

Beak: Short and stout, curving to a point.

Face: Surface smooth, skin fine and soft in texture.

Eyes: Large, round and prominent.

Wattles: Male - Non-Bearded: medium size, concave, nearly
round, fine in texture, free from wrinkles or folds. Bearded - very
small, concealed by beard, natural absence preferred. Female -
Non-Bearded: small, concave, forming a half circle, fine texture,
free from wrinkles or folds. Bearded: small to nonexistent,
concealed by beard.

Ear-Lobes: Male - Non-Bearded: small, oval, fine in texture, free
from wrinkles or folds. Bearded: very small, almost concealed by

muffs. Female: very small, rest of description the same as the male.

Crest: Male - medium size, soft and full. As upright as comb will permit, having a few silky feathers streaming gracefully backwards from the lower and back part of the crest. Female: medium size, soft and full, globular, upright, well balanced.

Head: Moderately small, short, carried so that a line drawn parallel with tip of the tail will bisect the comb.

Beard & Muffs: Bearded varieties - thick, full, extending back of eyes and projecting from sides of face and composed of feathers turned horizontally backwards, from both sides of the beak, from the center, vertically downwards, the whole forming a collar of three ovals in a triangular group, giving a muffed effect.

Neck: Short, gracefully arched, with a very full hackle flowing well over the shoulders.

Back: Male - short, broad from shoulders to saddle, quite rounded, its entire length rising gradually from middle of the back towards tail. Female - short, broad from shoulders to cushion, quite rounded its entire length, rising gradually from middle of back towards tail.

Saddle: Male - Rising from back at base of cape, very broad and round, plumage profuse and long, lower saddle feathers flowing over tips of wings and mingling with fluff.

Cushion: Rising from back at base of cape, very broad and round, plumage abundant.

Tail: Male - short, very shredded at ends, well spread at base, filled underneath with an abundance of soft feathers which are overlapped by coverts and lesser sickles, the whole forming a duplex curve with back and saddle. Sickles, lesser sickles, and coverts - abundant, soft, well curved, without hard quills, concealing main tail feathers. Female - short, very shredded at ends, well spread at base, filled underneath with an abundance of soft feathers which are overlapped by cushion and coverts, the whole forming a duplex curve with back and cushion.

Wings: Medium size, closely folded, carried well back and nearly horizontal, well above the lower thighs ending short of stern. Shoulders and fronts: concealed by hackles and breast feathers. Bows and coverts: Very well rounded. Primaries: medium length, well shredded, tapering convexly to stern, tips concealed by saddle feathers.

Breast: Carried forward, very full, well rounded and of great depth and width.

Body And Fluff: Body of moderate length, broad, deep and well rounded from breastbone to stern and let down well between the legs.

Legs and Toes: Male - Legs short and stout, set well apart, straight when viewed from the front. Lower thighs: short, stout at top, tapering to hocks, abundantly feathered. Hocks: covered with soft and silky feathers curving inwards about the hocks. Shanks: rather short, stout in boner, well feathered on the outer sides with silky plumage, the upper part growing out from thigh plumage and continuing into foot feathering. Spurs: medium size and length, set just above the 5th toe. Toes: five, the three front straight, well and evenly spread, the hind toe double, the normal toe in natural position and the extra toe placed above, starting from close to the other toe, but well formed, longer than the other toes and curving upwards and backwards; the outer and middle toe well feathered. Female - same as male except no spur. (Bare middle toe a serious defect in either sex)

Color: Bearded White Silkie

Male & Female: Comb, Face, Wattles: deep mulberry, approaching black.

Beak: Leaden blue
Eyes: black

Disqualifications:
* More or less than 5 toes
* Absence of beard or muffs.
* Shanks not feathered down outer sides
See APA Standard for Other DQs and cuts

Appendix II - Show Standard in the United Kingdom

(*Source*: The Silkie Club of Great Britain at www.thesilkieclub.co.uk , accessed May 2013.)

Classification : Large fowl light breed

Egg Colour : Tinted to cream

Origin : Asia

Silkie fowl have been mentioned by authorities for several hundred years. Some think that they originated in India, whilst others favor China and Japan. The Silkie is regarded as a light breed, and as such it must be exhibited. Its persistent broodiness is a breed characteristic, and either pure or crossed, the breed provides reliable broodies for the eggs of large fowl or bantams.

General Characteristics

MALE:
Carriage

- Stylish, compact and lively

Type

- Body – broad and stout looking.
- Back – short, saddle silky and rising to the tail.
- Stern – broad and abundantly covered with fine fluff, saddle hackles soft, abundant and flowing.
- Breast – broad and full, shoulders stout, square, and fairly covered with neck hackle.
- Wings – soft and fluffy at the shoulders, with the ends of the flights ragged and 'Osprey plumage; (i.e. some strands of the flights hang loosely downwards).

- Tail – short and very ragged at the end of the harder feathers of the tail proper. It should not be flowing, but forming a short round curve.

Head

- Short and neat.
- Good crest, soft and full, and as upright as the comb will permit, having a six to twelve soft silky feathers streaming gracefully backwards from the lower back part of the crest to a length of 3.75cm (1½in). The crest proper should not show any hardness of feather.
- Beak short and broad at the base.
- Eyes brilliant black, and not too prominent.
- Comb almost circular in shape, preferably broader than long, with a number of small prominences over it, and having a slight indentation or furrow transversely across the middle.
- Face smooth.
- Wattles concave, nearly semi-circular, and not long or pendant.
- Ear lobes more oval than round.
- Neck – short or medium length, broad and full at the base, with the hackles abundant and flowing.

Legs and feet

- Free from scales.
- Thighs wide apart and legs short.
- No hard feathers on the hocks, but a profusion of soft silky plumage is permissible.
- Thighs covered with abundant fluff. The feathers on the legs should be moderate in quantity.
- Toes five in number, with the fifth toe diverging from the fourth.
- The middle and the outer toes feathered, but these feathers should not be too hard.

Plumage

Very silky and fluffy, with a profusion of hair like feathers.

FEMALE

The saddle broad and well cushioned, with the silkiest of plumage, which should nearly smother the small tail, the ragged ends alone protruding and inclined to be 'Cochiny' in appearance.

- The legs are particularly short in the female, and the under and thigh fluff should nearly meet the ground.
- The head crest is short and neat, like a powder puff, with no hard feathers, and the eye should not be hidden by the crest, which should stand up and out, not split be the comb.
- Ear lobes small and roundish.
- Wattles either absent, or very small and oval in shape.
- Comb small.
- Other characteristics are as in the male, allowing for sexual differences.

Colour

- ***The White*** : Male and female plumage snow white.

- ***The Black*** : Male and female plumage black all over, with a green sheen in the male. A minimal amount of color in the hackle is permissible, but not desirable. The beak should be dark slate. Eyes black. Comb, face and wattles mulberry. Earlobes turquoise blue or mulberry, the former being preferable. Legs and feet lead. Nails blue white. Skin mulberry.

- ***The Blue*** : Male and female plumage an even shade of blue from head to tail.

- ***The Gold*** : Male and female plumage a bright even shade of gold throughout, with darker feathers in the tail of both sexes permissible.

- ***The Partridge*** : Male Head and crest dark orange. Breast and fluff black. Hackles orange / yellow, free from washiness, each feather having a clear black strip down the centre. Back and shoulders dark orange. Wing bar solid black. Primaries black, free from any white. Secondaries, outer web dark orange, inner web black, the dark orange alone showing when the wing is closed. Tail and sickles black. Leg and foot feather black. Under color slate grey, free from white.

Female Neck and breast lemon striped black. Hackle feathers black centre with lemon edge. Chest, lemon and black mingling. Body, including wings and cushion, black barring on soft partridge brown. Under color slate grey. Leg and foot feather color as body. Black permissible in the tail.

In all colors, with the exception of the black, the beak should be blue.

The Bearded Silkie

As a standard Silkie, but with clearly defined ear muff and beard.

The Bantam Silkie

Counterpart of large fowl in all respects.

Weights

Large Fowl : Male 1.8 1kg (4lbs) Female 1.36kg (3lbs)
Bantam Fowl : Male 600g (22ozs) Female 500g (18ozs)

Scale Of Points

- Type 20
- Head 30
- Legs 10
- Colour 10
- Plumage 30

Serious Defects

- Hard feathers.

- Green beak or tip to the beak.
- Horns protruding from the comb
- Ruddy comb wattles or face.
- Eye other than black.
- Incorrect color in plumage or skin.
- Plumage not Silky
- Want of crest 'Polish' or split crest – the crest should not hang over the eyes.
- Green soles to the feet.
- Any deformities, as listed in the Poultry Club Book of Standards, including crooked or turned toes and uneven wattles.

Disqualifications

- Single comb.
- Toes other than five in number.
- Green legs.
- Featherless legs or feet.
- Vulture hocks.

Glossary

American Poultry Association (APA) - The association in charge of setting standards for pure bred poultry in the United States. This group maintains the American Standard of Perfection, which outlines breed specifications for show poultry.

American Standard of Perfection - Published by the American Poultry Association, this book contains breed standards for recognized types of poultry in the United Stated.

Bantam - A term describing chicken or ducks that are small in size. Bantam chickens are generally $1/4^{th}$ the size of larger breeds. In America, they are sometimes referred to as Banty or Banties.

Barbicels - The small hook-like filaments on the barbules of a feather that give the structure rigidity and coherence.

Beak - The hard structure composing the nose and mouth of a chicken. Curved slightly and narrowing to a definite point.

Beard - Refers to a grouping of feathers situated just below the beak of a bird.

Bedding - Any material spread on the floor of a chicken coop. Most commonly used substances for bedding purposes are straw, various forms of hay and grasses, and wood chips or shavings.

Brood or broody - Refers to a hen's tendency to care for baby chicks. The same term applies to a group of chicks after they have hatched.

Brooder - A heated enclosure that is used to emulate the warmth that a mother hen will give her baby chicks. We often refer to a brooding area as the enclosure you will use when raising your chicks for the first 4-6 weeks. The brooding area is normally a well-bedded area with a heating lamp, food, and water.

Candle - The method used to examine an intact egg to determine if it has been fertilized.

Cape - Refers to the narrow feathers falling between a chicken's neck and back.

Clutch - Term referring to a group of eggs that are hatched either in a nest or an incubator. Can be used to refer to any group of eggs laid by one hen.

Coccidiosis - A disease found in birds and mammals that affects the intestines and is generally fatal.

Cock - A rooster or male chicken.

Cockerel - A rooster or male chicken under one year of age.

Comb - An outgrowth of skin on top of a chicken's head, which along with the wattles and beak are used by the bird to regulate its body temperature. Silkie chickens have a rose or cushion comb resembling a wart-like lump.

Commercial Feeds - Chicken feeds that are mixed by a manufacturer according to a published recipe and sold in retail settings.

Competition - In the context of poultry, a judged event where individual birds compete against one another to determine the degree to which they conform to recognized breed standards.

Coop - Any structure designed for the express purpose of housing chickens. A coop may or may not have an attached run or yard.

Crest - On crested breeds, a large puff of feathers sitting on top of the head.

Diapers - Sanitary clothing used to catch urine and feces. Used in human babies and in animals like chickens that cannot be successfully housebroken or litter trained.

Dirt Baths - The habit of chickens to roll in dirt to cool themselves, to remove excess oil from their feathers, and to control parasites.

Down - On newly hatched chicks, the soft feathers that have the feeling of fur. On adult birds, down is found under the main feathers, usually near the bottom or under the bird's wings. The feathers of adult Silkie chickens, due to their lack of barbicels, most closely resemble down.

Dusting - Refers to a chicken's habit of taking "dirt baths" to clean their feathers and repel parasites.

Hackles - A rooster's pointed neck feathers.

Hatchery - A commercial facility that exists to hatch out and sell baby chickens or other types of poultry and fowl.

Hatchability - Refers to the number or percentage of eggs in an incubator that hatch.

Limited Ranging - An arrangement of housing chickens where the birds are confined to a protected area, but with adequate space to move around in a yard for the purpose of foraging for food.

Marek's Disease - An infectious poultry disease caused by a herpes virus that attacks the nerves, causes paralysis, and results in the widespread formation of tumors.

Maturation - The time required for a baby of any species to grow and become an adult.

Molt - The process whereby a chicken sheds and re-grows its primary feathers.

Mycotoxins - A toxic substance produced by the growth of a fungus.

Mycoplasma - Parasitic, pathogenic microorganisms that lack a cell wall and are thus unaffected by common antibiotics.

Natural Hatching - The process whereby fertilized eggs are hatched out by a hen.

Nest - The area chosen by a hen to lay eggs.

Omnivore - An animal or person that eats foods of both animal and plant origin.

Pecking Order - Refers to the hierarchical social structure of a flock of chickens, which determines levels of aggression from the alpha chicken downward.

Perch - The elevated bar on which chickens sleep at night, also known as a roost.

Plumage - A bird's feathers.

Poultry - Birds, like chickens, that have been domesticated for their meat or eggs, or to serve as pets.

Pullet - A female chicken under one year of age.

Roost - The elevated bar on which chickens sleep at night, also known as a perch.

Rooster - The term for a male chicken, also known as a cock.

Saddle - The feathers on a chicken's back that point towards the rear.

Salmonella - A bacterium that occurs in the intestine and causes gastrointestinal distress commonly referred to as "food poisoning."

Scaly leg mite - A specific mite that burrows under the scales on the legs of a chicken causing swelling and crusty eruptions.

Setting - When a hen incubates her eggs she is said to be "setting" or "sitting."

Sexed - Sorting young chicks by gender, a process virtually impossible in Silkie chicks until they are 8 to 9 months in age.

Shank - The portion of a chicken's leg between the toes and the first leg joint.

Sickles - The pointed tail feathers present on a rooster.

Silkie Club of Great Britain – The official group that establishes breed standards for Silkie chickens in the UK.

Standard - A breed standard is an agreed upon description of the characteristics a bird must have to be considered an ideal example of its breed.

Starter or Starter Feed - Feed with a high concentration of protein specially formulated for newly hatched chicks.

Straight Run - A group of newly hatched chicks that have not been sorted by gender (sexed.)

Tractor - In reference to chickens, a "tractor" is a moveable chicken coop.

Vent - The outer opening of the cloaca through which a chicken passes eggs and excrement.

Works Cited

AmericanSilkieBantamClub.org

Anderson, M. *The Backyard Chickens Breed Guide*. Kindle Edition. 2013.

BackYardChickens.com

Damerow, Gail. *Storey's Guide to Raising Chickens: Care, Feeding, Facilities*. 3rd ed. North Adams, MA: Storey Publishing, 2010.

Heinrichs, Christine. *How to Raise Poultry*. Voyageur Press. Kindle Edition. 2009.

Jeffreys, Mel. *A Beginners Guide to Keeping Backyard Chickens: Breed Guide, Chicken Tractors & Coops, Hatching & Raising Chicks, Plus More*. Kindle Edition. 2013.

MyPetChicken.com

Percy, Pam. *Field Guide to Chickens*. Voyageur Press, 2006.

Ruppenthal, R.J. *Best Chicken Breeds: 12 Types of Hens That Lay Lots of Eggs, Make Good Pets, and Fit in Small Yards*. Kindle Edition. 2012.

Ruppenthal, R.J. *Backyard Chickens for Beginners*. Kindle Edition. 2012.

The Silkie Club of Great Britain at www.thesilkieclub.co.uk

Willis, Kimberley and Rob Ludlow. *Raising Chickens For Dummies*. Hoboken, NJ: Wiley Publishing, Inc., 2009.

CPSIA information can be obtained
at www.ICGtesting.com
Printed in the USA
BVOW08s0627040118
504322BV00002B/230/P